LYDIA LUNCH

interviews by V. Vale

PUBLISHERS/EDITORS: V. Vale, Marian Wallace
COVER PHOTO: V. Vale
BOOK DESIGN: Marian Wallace

RE/Search copy editors, staff & consultants
    Patrick Kwon
    Elsa Kim
    Cathryn Moothart
    Andrew Bishop
    Emily Dezurick-Badran
    Robert Collison
    Britton Nasser
    Emily Rose
    Elizabeth Edwards
    Angie de Leon
    Gary Chong
    David Coons
    Gail Takamine
    Andrea Reider

RE/Search Publications
20 Romolo Place #B
San Francisco, CA 94133
(415) 362-1465
info@researchpubs.com
www.researchpubs.com

Opposite page: "Blow Me Away" by Lydia Lunch

L YDIA LUNCH is a polymath autodidact whose *oeuvre* encompasses virtually all of the Seven Arts (and then some). As one of the inventors of the NO WAVE movement in New York City circa 1976–1977, she inaugurated her band Teenage Jesus and the Jerks with strict attention to precise rhythms, breaks, and space. Their songs are overlaid with screaming vocals and bottleneck guitar, underpinned by thunderous bass. Minimalist, yet powerful.

A relentless collaborator and facilitator who is quick to seize any chance opportunity or encounter, Ms. Lunch has expressed herself in writing, songwriting, acting in films, producing art photography and video, gallery installations, Spoken Word, (anti-) poetry, (anti-) theater, and magazine/book editing/publishing. She has contributed interviews, essays, and prefaces to a host of publications. *And we* recommend her enlightening cookbook, *The Need to Feed.*

For the past decade Lydia Lunch has lived in Barcelona, Spain, enjoying ready access to the amazing architectural creations of Antonio Gaudi, RE/Search's favorite architect. She periodically tours Europe and America performing music and Spoken Word, including a 2009 resurrection of Teenage Jesus and the Jerks. Another recent musical project is a collaboration with Cypress Grove.

Most of the interviews here are transcribed from two *Counter Culture Hour* video episodes, produced by Marian Wallace at RE/Search headquarters; the other conversations were taped before or after Lydia's San Francisco club dates. Lydia is scathingly funny, punning, savagely deprecating and mercilessly sardonic, as she levies salvos at America, describes supplanting Orwell's "Big Brother" concept with her "Big Sister" archetype, and claims the throne as the female J.G. Ballard. She may have the darkest sense of humor on the planet. Search for her live performances on YouTube, and for up-to-date information on what Lydia has been up to, go to *www.lydia-lunch.org.*

■ VALE: Welcome to *The Counter Culture Hour*. I'm your host, V. Vale. I've been doing counter-culture publishing since 1977, with *Search and Destroy*, which documented the Punk Rock Cultural Revolution, and *RE/Search,* which continued that wonderful tradition.

Today we have Lydia Lunch. She was an original Punk Rock progenitor, actually, in New York City. She is an artist of extremely varied accomplishments. So welcome, Lydia Lunch. This is *The Counter Culture Hour;* so I'm trying to keep it to that penumbra, or whatever you want to call it—

■ LYDIA LUNCH: *Good luck...* From the time I was ten—maybe eleven—in Rochester, up-state New York ... I was born in 1959, so we'll say by 1969 or '71, I already knew I had to get out of there!

As a young child, what influenced me very much was actually 1967, at the age of eight, when there were riots going on right outside my *front door.* There were riots in Rochester, Detroit, Cleveland—a lot of race riots were happening. And since that happened right outside my front door, even though I'm *eight...* the bizarre incident is that I was watching *The Haunting,* based on a Shirley Jackson book, *The Haunting of Hill House* as the riots were happening. So, I'm having two kinds of fierce stimuli coming at me! But, the riot caused such joy and elation in me that it counteracted the fear of the film, which is still a terrifying horror film.

So, as the riots are raging and I noticed my father's station wagon getting smashed to s—t, I'm like *cheering for joy*—I just can't believe it. I hear black voices screaming and I see people running down the streets; it's violence, pande-monium, and chaos... and even in my twisted, eight-year-old mind I was just *joyful*—I didn't know what the hell it was, but I was happy it was going on.

Also entering my psyche (and I think because

I was so excited), I remember my father saying, "That's *it*—go to your room! Get out of here!" And when you go to your room at eight, let's remember that Top Forty radio was The Doors, Jefferson Airplane, James Brown—I didn't realize this until recently, but these were songs of protest and drugs and free love... but even then it starts turning a little uglier, as I get a little older. As things like "Riders on the Storm" or "The End"... as culture, music, pop culture turns *darker,* this is somehow impregnating my psychic fabric; no doubt.

Then literature comes in, at twelve. From reading *Last Exit to Brooklyn* [Hubert Selby, Jr.] at twelve, thirteen—that was really the first conscious thrust, for me to know that I had to get out of where I was, and that I had to do it *artistically.* So, it really wasn't music; I think it was *literature.* With the readings of Selby, de Sade, Miller, and Genet at a very early age—I didn't even know how these books fell into my lap, probably just the used bookstore—that's what told me, through some format of the truth and real life experiences, that you could take what you knew or how it affected you... and go *somewhere else* with it.

I think by then the *music* came in too—but we're talking like, *glam.* We're talking Bowie, The Stooges, Lou Reed—this comes in. Rock concerts at the age of thirteen, these big Rock concerts which I was allowed to go to—I mean, that was *it:* the culmination of the riots, literature, and then music...

By fourteen I had run away to New York City. Now that's 1973, but the Ramones' first album came out not long after that. We forget the Ramones were pretty early on, *and* the New York Dolls, and that's what drove me to New York as a fourteen-year-old runaway. Now, I didn't stay there for very long—I was only *fourteen,* I couldn't figure out exactly how to... I had to go back upstate, get a job, lie about my age, get some money, and then at *sixteen,* that was *it*—I was out of there.

At that point, there was no Punk Rock. I mean, there was Patti Smith, there was Television, there were the Heartbreakers, and I think Richard Hell's first show hadn't been till after I was living in New York. So, I went there at sixteen and it wasn't Punk, it wasn't *anything.* Certainly the music had a pull: Patti Smith, Television—it had a pull to me in the sense that I thought it was still too *traditional*—I had to go there and kick some dirt up!

I didn't know how I was going to do it. I would corner people like Lenny Kaye and shout my poems in their face. And he was the only one that would listen to them, because I was this brash, loud-mouth, tiny *terror,* and people were just like "What?"—they didn't *want* to know. Like: David Byrne would run away from me, Richard Hell would run away from me… they were horrified, antagonized, they didn't know *what* to do, they didn't know how to deal and it was really only Lenny Kaye that would listen.

Then I saw Suicide, and they became my best friends. Suicide, to me, was *it,* because what had influenced me musically when I got to New York—by the time I got there—I had rejected as *too traditional.* Suicide was one of the first shows, and I said: "That's exactly what it's all about."

I don't define Suicide as "Punk"—I define Suicide totally in their own category. I mean: it's something that didn't have a definition at the time. They were one of the first [bands] doing electronic music that was very ugly, yet there was still some kind of beauty or sexuality involved. You have this guy in a wig and leather jacket, smashing himself in the face with a microphone and then threatening all ten of the audience—that was *heaven*. So then I knew I had come to the right place [laughs]... it had nothing to do with Punk.

Another thing is, when I first landed in New York as a sixteen-year-old runaway with no money, no place to live, there was a club I had read about on 21st Street called "Mothers," so I went there and some hippies picked me up. They were living in this loft on 24th Street, which is not far from Max's Kansas City. Kitty Bruce, Lenny Bruce's daughter, was just moving out and they said I could take her space. I was just this young runaway—I think they had *designs* on me, but that ended within the first day—like, "Nah!" [sneers]

Anyway, I dug my way into this loft not far from Max's Kansas City, so it was just a few blocks away and that's how Suicide became one of the first shows I saw there. As a sixteen-year-old with no money, I guess it was just easy to go to Max's and say, "Let me in!" and they *would*. Of course, you knew about Max's Kansas City because there were magazines like *Rock Scene* or *Creem* or *Circus*—

these magazines would come to upstate New York, so I already knew these places existed and that's where you'd go—you just beeline, it's *instinct*. I met James Chance not long after that, so this was pretty soon after arriving in New York.

To me, the period that I hit New York was really, at the end of... I don't really know what to call it... The "Post-Hippie" era: you know, Patti Smith, Television... These were groups that were definitely breaking from tradition, but still too traditional for what I was seeking, even if they had inspired me *at first*. By the time I got there; by the time I was fifteen, sixteen, I was rejecting everything that inspired me—just instinctively—for being *too traditional*. It was *too Rock 'n' Roll,* and I wasn't interested in that; I needed something that was going to be far more *primal*.

It seemed easier to do music at the time. One of the first No Wave bands—which is really the movement I'm out of, which had nothing to do with Punk Rock; the first No Wave band that I saw was MARS. All of them had come out of St. Petersburg, Florida—which was where Exene Cervenka and Mark Pauline came out of, and Arto Lindsay and

Mark Cunningham who went on to have DNA and… all these people had came out of the St. Petersburg scene and ended up in New York for some strange reason. I don't know how I fell into that clique, exactly, but I think it was through Mars.

So, I saw Mars for the first time. You just saw a poster advertised; they were called "China" then; they looked weird. They're playing at CBGB's, they're one of the most perverse things you've ever seen… It sounds like insanity on stage, they look insane, the lead singer is making very bizarre faces and doesn't know he's doing it—and that to me was heaven. It wasn't long after seeing Mars that I said, "That's it—I have to do *music* to get my point across." I went from thinking I'd do poetry or Spoken Word to deciding, after seeing Mars and Suicide, that it had to be a *musical format* that was going to house my primal necessity: to scream and shout about my personal agony.

I took piano lessons for about three months as a child, but I just threw that out. I still love to play piano, though. I did an instrumental record where I played the piano and the guitar with Connie Burg of Mars, which we did in the mid-eighties—we did an instrumental record called *The Drowning of Lucy Hamilton* (which is one of her alter egos), which became the soundtrack to *The Right Side of My Brain,* the film I did with Richard Kern.

With Connie I recorded my only instrumental record where I play the piano—my only musical training—but I only know one song, and it just lasts forever.

The only way my parents encouraged me was—for some perverse reason they were so guilty about my family life... I had four kids in my family, I had an older sister by ten years and then a younger brother and a younger sister. But, because I was so smart and wily and they were so guilty, they started taking me to Rock concerts at age twelve and dropping me off. I remember saying to my mother at thirteen, "I need to go to this concert; it's for my *career!*" And she said, "What career?" "Now, what do you think, Mom?" But I knew, then, that I had to go to these concerts for my career. So, that's the only way they encouraged me: by really giving me free reign. I was the only child in my family to have free reign, because my grades were so good in school—because I was so manipulative, because I was

A RE/Search Pocketbook

the favorite. The others were on permanent lockdown. My father would pick me up at 2 a.m. from Rock concerts, at twelve, thirteen, fourteen, for my career—see how far that's gotten me now, hmm?

So, no, they didn't encourage anything. All of what I've done has been *in spite of* my parents. From the time I was twelve, I lived in the basement or the attic to be away from my family… then running away at fourteen, and then out of the house at fifteen or sixteen… I didn't have much contact. That's why one of the first songs I wrote with Teenage Jesus was called "Orphans"… and eventually that became true and it was wonderful.

■ V: What do you mean?

■ LL: Well, when you spend the first years of your childhood hating your parents, when they die, it's a great relief… if you've made peace with their failings and shortcomings. I always felt like so much of an outsider, so alienated, so alone—but not lonely, I never felt lonely…

This also goes with all of the movements that I've been involved in. As a child I always felt outside of everything. I lived outside of my family; I felt alienated in the best possible way.

Books were my friends. I had friends, but they didn't impact me as much as the writing of Hubert Selby. No one I knew had as deep an impact. And the people I knew that had as deep an impact were probably strange men whose cars I would get into—and *that's* where my story-telling career began, actually: in a strange man's car.

So, I think that through the words of other people, through literature, and through my natural alienation that carried on—even through the No Wave scene, being involved with all the bands of that period, going on to work with as many collaborators as I have throughout the twenty-eight years of my career—I still feel

"Casualty" by Lydia Lunch

completely outside of every movement. I don't feel pigeonholed into any movement; geographically I'm always on the move; collaboratively, I'm always looking for new collaborators, and I've always felt completely outside of any movement...happily.

Punk had a fashion that helped define "Punk," in a sense. You could tell who was Punk by the way they looked—a lot of it had to do with fashion. With No Wave that wasn't so: people just looked like *bums;* they looked poor, they looked insane, they were artists (a lot of them), so their clothes were not Punk decorated with colors, but just *shabby.* There was no style, there was *no visual style to No Wave* which is what made it very interesting because...

In order for people to be attracted to music that's so dissident—even within its own clique it has nothing to do with each other—this is really drawing on disparate elements. The only way to define No Wave is that it sounds like nothing you've ever heard before, probably not even like the other groups within the movement. When you hear Punk Rock you know it's Punk Rock. When you *see* Punk Rock it's very obvious: you know who's a

Punker and who isn't.

So, to me, I came out of a movement that was more defined by what it *wasn't*... more defined by the fact that it was not melodic, it did not use chords, it was only connected by how disconnected it was, by how dissident it was, by how discordant it was. And that's part of how negativity—*positive negativity* [!]—helped to really define *what* I would create, and *how* I have created. Taking a very negative situation which, for me, was the trauma of my birth, the trauma of being born, the trauma of religion and poverty in the nuclear family (which is a microcosm of fascism), in the inner city ghetto, and using all that negativity positively, even if it doesn't *sound* positive—because it's a primal scream ridden with hatred, anger, and angst.

Well, I'm smiling now and I was always smiling underneath it all, you know? I thought I was the great, unsung comedian, but I just don't allow people the punch line. I don't allow people the pause a punch line deserves, in order to feel the relief that a real comedian gives, because it's not my job to provide relief—it's my job to articulate frustration.

▮ V: It's *one* of your jobs—

■ LL: Not to give a solution, but to antagonize the problem, to articulate the problem. I've never been a solutionist—I don't think that's my duty. It's the same when I feel that I am almost this Brother Theodore-type comedian... and even *he* would allow for the punch line, for the laugh, for the relief. But I don't think that's my duty.

I've always been stubborn and I think... we all come out of terrible situations; whether it's just poverty or whatever type of abuse or trauma, it's just a political overhang of abuse that we *all* suffer now. I view history as a farce in the sense that it constantly repeats itself, nothing ever changes, we're almost *feudal,* this cycle—is it a cycle or is it just the same? Is it just a reincarnation of the same abuse of power that will always continue under the patriarchy?

I mean, with this kind of overview, no matter how horrible the situation becomes... or even if there's a *lull* in how horrible the situation is—for instance, under the Clinton years there seemed to be a lull in the damage done to the individual: socially, economically, intellectually, culturally. I always view the times we live in as so medieval, so feudal... which is so ridiculous: the patriarchy. The more that we understand the point of this endless war that has been waged from America outward for more than two [decades]—the more light and joy it brings into my life... not because I feel like the "No Wave Nostradamus"... but I just believe that *my stubbornness brings me more joy,* the older I get!

In a sense, I'm living in my own utopian creative wonderland outside of everyone and everything else, almost like the spy who geographically hops from location to location... playing with my friends wherever they may be, creating whatever I want to create—only because I've remained stubbornly independent, and have no restrictions on what I do placed upon me by anyone or anything, especially not even *budgetary.* Because... I will always find a way to create. And that's the beauty of why it always comes back to Spoken Word for me. I will always find a way to express the dilemma that many of us live under... and that brings me joy because that is my duty... that is my social calling. Look, computers crash, technology dies, but you can always afford a pencil.

▋ V: Or your own voice.

■ LL: You can always just tell the story. [Puts on strained, nasally voice] And eventually I might be talking through a tracheotomy box, but that's okay because I'll sound f—-n better!

To just think that for me, the more I understood how circular everything is, and the cycles—not only of time, of history, of life, of birth, of death, of growth, of whatever—the more I understood how cyclical everything is, the easier it just became for me to deal with it, and the more stubborn I became in order to represent my hysteria, my version of hysteria and history, and to continue documenting it.

▮ V: Wait a minute, that's a loaded word: "hysteria." What do you mean by it?

■ LL: Well, hysteria means "from the womb."

▮ V: Oh?

■ LL: I know. So… my hysteria—the hysteria of our times. Maybe it's fear of a female planet after all, which is continuing this ridiculous anarchy that comes out from America and is foisted on other nations.

At nine, I think, I turned to one of these huge golden Bibles that my father had sold as one of his door-to-door salesman ruses... These beautiful Bosch-esque depictions of heaven and hell... and as a nine-year-old who's only semi-conscious, you put yourself right into those flames. And I think that I was about nine or ten when I realized that religion was a farce: there was no salvation, there was no savior on the other side, there was no heaven or hell—this is *purgatory;* it's what you make it.

I think by ten I had crawled out from under the religious abuse that... It wasn't forced upon me, I didn't go to Catholic school, it's not as if my parents were religious—my father wasn't. So, between this twenty-pound Bible on my lap and my father playing canasta and drinking and gambling and dog-running, having his little German mafioso, it's like: you gotta find the truth somewhere between god and the devil. The truth, I guess... must exist.

With literature, with my horror fixation, with the escapism into murder fantasies, with a deadening of emotion to deal with trauma, with a flat-lining... Born into victimhood, you have few different ways of dealing with it. I think that my way of dealing with it, at a very early age, was basically by flat-lining my emotions.

▮ V: That means—

■ LL: That means *numb.* So, when you become cautious enough to figure out you have a few choices here, and anger, of course, is one... with anger there's a re-dilating of your emotions: either you're hysterically angry, or you're flat-lining. You flat-line when you try to control that which you have no control over—which is your situation. I think that once I gained, or *attempted* to gain control of my emotions... so that I wasn't further battered by the abuse of other people or the situation, or even more general over-sensitivity to the *real* situation we all live under... that part of my rebellion was to force myself into positions that would probably frighten other people horribly...

▮ V: Getting into cars with strange men—

■ LL: Well, I think—*yes.* My first storytelling episode: when I was twelve years old and got into the car with someone on a very snowy, blizzard-y day in upstate New York, in front of an x-rated movie theatre where I was waiting for the bus after school. After he'd circled the block three times, it was still snowing, there was no bus, it's freezing cold, and it's the dead of winter, it's four o'clock, it's getting dark, and someone offers me a ride and I decide: *finally.*

I knew that someone who circles the block three times, you don't get in the car with, unless you think you're going to be able to control the situation—or you don't care. It's not like I didn't know what the situation was here… and I think, taking the chance on that car ride—which culminated with me having a shotgun to my face as I was forced to tell stories about my sisters, gruesome stories in order to save my life, for which I was then paid and allowed to go… and then gave the perpetrator my phone number—I think pretty much ended any fear I had about anything, and it started my foray into story-telling.

▌V: You saved your life through story-telling—

■ LL: I saved my life through telling the right kind of story to the wrong kind of person. And I think after that point, I knew my power and where my powers lay.

Words were always what I wanted to work with. I mean, I was writing from the age of twelve—I was writing in notebooks, I was writing…

▌V: Your parents didn't encourage you?

■ LL: No. I would read my mother poems like "Kill Your Parents"! I couldn't believe I would force it upon her at twelve—*oh, very nice*—I'm sure she was horrified. I didn't need encouragement, I wasn't looking for encouragement, I never was looking for encouragement, I was never looking for applause or attention like that. It never mattered to me—never.

And, as a matter of fact, when I got to the age of twenty or so, when I found out that I did something that got too much of the wrong attention—which was a *positive* attention—I quit. When what I was doing with 8-Eyed Spy suddenly became very popular, I aborted. I couldn't stand it; I thought I didn't want people looking at me for the wrong reasons, thinking that they see something in me that they're fabricating... I just didn't want them to like me for the *wrong reasons*. I didn't want them to think that they found something that they could *relate to*—if you *really* knew, you'd be running out of the room, pal!

There *are some* people that can relate to me; that's why Spoken Word is so important to me... because it minimizes who's going to take their time to go to a show. I mean, Spoken Word is for a minority already. Then, when you're dealing with real-life facts and trauma, and you're not "entertaining" (and if it's entertaining, it's by *default* because you're dealing with trying to get to the bottom, to the *root* of some of these traumas), I mean, you're just whittling the audience down in droves anyway!

So, forming words and then Teenage Jesus and the Jerks, where the music was still there as a fascist rhythm to back up the primal scream of the angst of the words—of that hatred; of the anger... And it wasn't long after being in New York that I started doing Spoken Word and the first piece I did was called "Daddy Dearest," so I went right to the *core* with Spoken Word. I got it right on the table with the first piece, because I knew that so much of what was driving me was my hatred

"Survival" by Lydia Lunch

and anger: first, against my father; and then against men in positions of power.

We start with the father, then the father of the country, then God the Father and it just grew from there; it starts with one man and then, you know, they're all guilty! (Well, they're not *all* guilty, but there are certainly a lot of guilty ones that are men.) So, I think, starting with a piece called "Daddy Dearest"—that was the first performance I ever did live of Spoken Word. Why I was able to do that, I guess, was: I was in my early twenties— this was pre-Jerry Springer and all that crap where everyone's trauma gets laid on the table like so many drying bloodstains. I knew that my trauma, no matter what it was, was not unique. I knew that *pain* was the universal driving force of so many people—I knew that only in the *details* was it specific, and I just found it urgent to cut right to the chase and get right to the point...

That was called "Daddy Dearest": an open letter to my father, which ends with a scream-ing tirade of hatred, then "Love, Lydia" just to add the contradiction which has been part of my *forte*. Because, I think first and foremost, I am the ultimate contradiction and a contrarian to boot; this is part of the territory I inhabit: I embrace my contradictions. When you start out young hating men—hating your father—but then you become promiscuous and sex-endorsing—sexually voracious—then that's already a contradiction you have to deal with. I think what I do is try to understand, better, *contradictory emotions*—how to live with them.

▮ V: How to live with your own—

■ LL: Well, not only my own... I'm not the *only one* who's full of contradictions! I think that the problem with society is that "they" try to pigeonhole us, into being this, into being that, into being this way, having *this* belief. *Extreme individuals* are full of contradictions.

I don't know who coined the term "Spoken Word." I know I started calling what I was doing "Spoken Word" very early on, but I didn't know if the term existed before that. I don't know if it just slipped out of my mouth or where it came from. It's just: why I liked it was because it said *nothing*. When you say "spoken word," in a sense that's what it is, but *what* is it? When you say "performance," I never felt that what I did was Performance Art, because I felt that Performance Art used words and theatrics and props and stage setting. And what *I* wanted to do was just strip it down to the most basic form, which is *extreme storytelling*: an emotional exchange; subjects dealing with political trauma, and an extreme expression of that. Well, it's just bizarre to me that there aren't *more* people doing it now than there were then, really. I don't consider poetry and "poetry slams" the same as Spoken Word; I consider them very, very different.

▌ V: How so?

■ LL: Well... First of all, it's just the nature of *poetry:* there's short sound stabs... poetry is just a very *specific* format and I think Spoken Word is developing a *longer* story—you have to be able to hold people's attention through an emotional roller-coaster. A poem is very short and specific; I mean, you can do twenty poems in a session—if they don't like one poem, well, maybe the next one will catch them... and, it also has to be *catchy.*

Spoken Word does not have to be catchy; you have to be able to seduce people with your language, with the rhythm, with what you're talking *about.* I think it's a very, very different format.

I specialize in doing longer pieces—sometimes just one long piece, one long speech or one long story—*that's* what I specialize in. And I think other people, even like Rollins or Jello Biafra or Exene Cervenka or Nicole Blackman or Michelle Tea or Daphne Gottlieb—they still use more… if not poetry forms, their pieces are broken up into small, incidental sections that maybe are strung together without necessarily a connective tissue.

Maybe there is a connective tissue. Maybe with, like, Jello, it's gonna be about politics, for instance. With Rollins, it's gonna be about day-to-day incidentals and cultural commentary; with Exene, she seems to marry the political, the day-to-day, and social commentary. What *I* do is either pretty much a straight political piece which is a tirade, attacking the enemy with as much emotion or as many facts as I can. Or, for instance, what I did last time at the Café Du Nord and what I'll be doing tonight at the Hemlock: telling more specific, very long stories, about either myself or certain people, filled with the details that I hope create a better understanding of this kind of dilemma which the individuals find themselves in… without giving a *solution*.

▮ V: Heaven forbid that—

■ LL: It's not my job. I don't know what the
solution is. You keep living; there is no solution. *The solution to life is death; it'll get here!*
There's no solution; if you don't like something, you change it; if you don't like yourself,
you change it; if you don't like where you live,
you change it… it doesn't seem so complicated
to *me!*

My style: I've been dying my hair since the
time I was thirteen: black or black-cherry, or
red, blue—I don't mean "Punk blue," I mean
blue-black. I already was wearing too much
make-up and I already had a sense of style, a
lot of it influenced by music. But I wouldn't
dress like the music that I was drawn to, because I didn't want to wear silver and—
▮ V: Gold—
■ LL: Gold. So, I had a harsh look. I think it
was more just "witchy." I always had this
witchy thing going on and then it just "trans-
lated" when I went to New York. Also, I was
very poor. I mean, you go to New York with
nothing—I went with like one small bag. So
the clothes you have, you'd better like them because you're going to be wearing them all the
time, because you're not gonna get any more.
So I tried it down there wearing a wet look

[vinyl] dress. But for some reason, I had a more defined style than the other people in No Wave because I wasn't dressing like an art school student—again, in their impoverished rags, their pauper's clothes. *Clothes* weren't the issue; I had a sense of style because I dyed my hair, I was cute, and I wore lipstick.

You just didn't need that much money. I think the first apartment I had in New York was like seventy-five bucks a month, on 12th Street between Avenues A and B, but it was a building that was a back building and both buildings on either side were burnt down and there was garbage six feet high between the front and back buildings. The guy who had been there before had been electrocuted by his TV and his dog ate his face off, so the place stunk of death.

I needed this apartment because it was seventy-five dollars. I don't even know how I got the seventy-five dollars… they didn't want me to see it, but I said, "Look, I know someone died there—let me take care of it!" And I went to the nearest *botanica* and got some kind of black bottle with a skull on it, which eliminated the smell of death when nothing else would. But my apartment was seventy-five dollars and I guess then I got a boyfriend and sent *him* to work! I don't know, but it wasn't hard to make a hundred dollars a month—*then*.

The only job I had for a few weeks—which was how I got my name "Lydia Lunch"—was working at a bar, while I was underage, stealing food for Mink DeVille, who were like my second friends in New York. And one day, walking home with food that I had stolen for them because we're all starving to death, Willy DeVille—and this is before Teenage Jesus—just says, "Lydia Lunch!" I wouldn't have chosen this name—it sounds like a porno name. I didn't even have a band yet, but it just stuck and it was just *there,* I couldn't get rid of it—but it was from feeding my poor friends with a job I had for two weeks.

Then you do like most of the women or men: you try to do some kind of sex work that wasn't too taxing, whether it was working a few days or a few weeks at a go-go bar or cocktail bar—whatever. That's how I took Teenage Jesus to Europe for the first time—I took them to England by working at a go-go bar as a cocktail waitress for a few months, because I knew we *had* to go to England. By that time, there was really something going on in England, and that's where the Punk thing was starting—not New York, because New York was No Wave. We weren't interested in Punk Rock—at least no one I knew was interested in Punk; we thought it was ridiculous, it was redundant.

That's at first; when it started, it was a fashion statement. In San Francisco it was defined as "Punk" just because everyone was the outsiders, as you said. In New York, first there was No Wave; Punk didn't come to New York until later. We'd heard about Punk in England. I don't know who the first Punk band in New York was—you could consider it the Ramones, but the Ramones were really *before* Punk.

▮ V: I thought they started as early as 1974.

▪ LL: They did… maybe as early as '73.

▮ V: Yeah, maybe '73, and even Patti Smith, too—

▪ LL: To me, even though the Ramones became the definitive "Punk," it's not what it first seemed to be. And the Dead Boys were also one of the first bands, from Cleveland—but they were really more like The Stooges than Punk.

We could go back and say that The Stooges were really the first Punks. We could go back and say the Velvet Underground were really the first Punks, but it depends on how you define "Punk." See, I define what I did as *outside* of the Punk category, because to me, No Wave, like the Dadaists, at least in New York, made more sense to me, because we were only connected, once more, by that which we did *not* have in common. We were connected by the fact that we *didn't* sound alike, we were connected by the fact that we *didn't* look alike, we were connected by the fact that we came from all different parts, scattered—and culminated here. And a lot of people from that movement,   that they then brought to the music, to the movement.

If we were just talking about *No New York* [the album], within that, every band is very different, because: the Contortions are funk; Teenage Jesus is just fascist rhythm, with very orchestrated noise and very precise [stop-and-starts]. Teenage Jesus was one of the tightest operations at that time because they were beaten if they made mistakes... because we didn't want to sound amateurish. We didn't want to sound "musical," but we had to sound *precise* because when you're dealing with something so simple as this kind of rhythm-based, non-melodic, primal scream, it had to be *tight*. We rehearsed a lot. Mars had a more lugubrious, almost *ectoplasmic* sound; and DNA was not funk but a rhythmic and very "awkward" sound.

■ V: Yeah, jagged.

■ LL: Very jagged. So within [the *No New York* album], it was very different. Again, the connective tissue was this *discordance,* maybe aggressiveness, although I would say that Mars was more of this *sinuous insanity,* so I

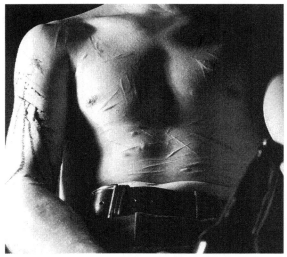

"When Words Fail" by Lydia Lunch

don't know...

■ V: Who coined this term "No Wave"?

■ LL: Well, people have blamed me for it, but I don't know if I did. I think I named the album "No New York" but I don't know. I don't know if I coined it, or who coined it, but it made sense to me because I was against everything, basically. I was anti-everything, I was *anti-all movements*. I was anti- what inspired *me,* I was rebelling against all tradition.

I was even, again, as the outsider status, rebelling within my collective. Within my own creativity, I was rebelling against *that,* because I had Teenage Jesus, and at the same time I had another band, Beirut Slump, and they sounded exactly the opposite. I had Teenage Jesus, which was sharp, fast, sound stabs of precise noise; and then Beirut Slump, which someone once described as a "slug crawling over a razor blade." So, I was not only rebelling against whatever influenced me, but, creatively, from the get-go, I was rebelling against *myself.*

Then, post that [was] 8-Eyed Spy, which rebelled against *this* because it was more like pop, rock, surf, chaos. After that, Queen of Siam, which was big band, nursery rhyme. So this is why I might not be the best person to speak about "community," because I was trying to unify my own schizophrenia or find vehicles for it. No wonder I always felt alone! I'm living in a nut house, all of us. Alone—I don't think so.

But I think No Wave came before New Wave.

▌ V: Yeah.

■ LL: So there you go, it came before New Wave, because again, New Wave (as you said) was the commodified version [of Punk]. And that was really more bands like Blondie, even though Blondie existed *before,* but they were commodified as New Wave, when they could play their instruments proficiently enough to record their horrible little pop ditties.

Well, I played guitar and I wrote the music for Teenage Jesus and I wrote the music for Beirut Slump and I played guitar for that and I played guitar in Queen of Siam and I did an instrumental record with guitar and piano.

▌ V: How did you learn?

■ LL: I didn't learn. I just... it wasn't about *learning,* it was about using music or the guitar as a *tool to back up the words.* Now, if the words are the *priority,* which they were—then

I knew that the words, being as angry as they were, had to come out like a primal scream, a staccato primal scream. Someone gave me a guitar—it wasn't even a six-string guitar. They gave me like a broken four-string guitar at first, and that's how I wrote the music for Teenage Jesus.

Then I developed my slide technique, which is really my definitive sound. It's a specific slide technique; it was just instinctual—I didn't learn it. We rehearsed, chronically, in Teenage Jesus. Because I felt it really necessary that if we were going to make music and the drums—well it sounds *plural* but we only had *one* drum... and that was by *insistence*. I only wanted a snare and one cymbal, because I felt that if you're pounding out a rhythm that's just "aaa aaa aaa aaa," why do you need more?

"Less is more" was the whole theory behind what I did, anyway. It was about the voice, and about the words, and about the guitar. It was a primal, battering beat. I had technique, but it was instinct and it was just about rehearsing to get it right... and that's all. And it had to be very precise. But within that precise nature, there was the horribly-slicing slide guitar, which defined the sound.

So, it was just about instinct… and it was about rehearsing enough to get it right. Instinct, nothing else. No lessons, no one taught me. I don't even think I had a guitar during some of the first gigs of Teenage Jesus—I had to borrow a guitar. But, I knew that I needed a Fender tube amp and preferably a Fender guitar. Now *how* I knew this, I don't know, but it was the most trebly and slicing sound.

So, it was about knowing what it had to sound like, and getting an instrument to do that. I was called "one of the greatest guitar players in the world" by Lester Bangs, but he's *dead*. I still play the guitar and I still play piano. My last performance actually playing guitar was with Nels Cline, one of the most amazing guitar players of modern composition, because *he* requested I do a concert with him on guitar. But anyone *less*—I mean, there's no reason. I've made my point with the guitar.

▌V: Did you use standard or open tuning?

■ LL: I used standard tuning, because again, it wasn't about the tuning, it wasn't about playing chords, it was more about the rhythm. The songs were very precise—all instinct.

∎ V: The kind of great thing about that time was that everyone had permission to try things out like that.

■ LL: Everyone *still* has permission to do whatever they want—they're just too damned lazy to actually get up and *do* it. Or they're jaded, or everything's been done; they don't wanna leave their house, or they sit behind their computer. Who took away *permission?* No one *gave* permission and no one's taken it away! It's nonsense. I mean, why...

We can blame—and I do—MTV, for groups in their early twenties sounding like groups did thirty years ago and dressing like them and saying and doing nothing new. However, it's not that anyone has granted, given away, or taken permission—it's just that those who commodify it are looking for a certain genre that is commodified. These young robots have no vision of their own: You don't have vision, you don't give it a sound. That's been my theory. But ultimately, do whatever you want! I don't care because I'm not giving or taking away permission.

I'm very much encouraged, just by the people I know who exist. That they exist and that I know, even if it's not collected—there *is* a collective, even if they're not in close contact with each other. I feel that there is a scattered community, even if it's not connected by regular meetings or... Some of my friends I won't see for another five years; a lot of it has to do with geography.

From a very early point in my career, I managed to get my groups to England, to Europe, which has always been more culturally adventurous for supporting diverse artists and not wanting to pigeonhole them, and allowing them performance spaces and opportunities. Somehow, instinctively, I learned that at a very early age. Getting Teenage Jesus to England and to Germany made a big impact, because of the name, because of the time, because of the music.

Forcing myself, over and over again, to go to Europe, has allowed me to continue carrying on as an independent artist, where a lot of people who I know (or "grew up" with at the same time), didn't make that choice, or didn't have the wherewithall to figure out how to get to Europe. I always had the broader picture that *that's* where I needed to go, because it was going to be more supportive, artistically—and it is and it has been.

But yes, my friends have been more scattered. I take great comfort in the fact that individuals do exist—even if we're not in a collective yearly Burning Man cooperative somewhere. Although I wish we could all be, we aren't. But I feel like I'm the one that *tries*. I'm the gypsy that's always traveling around to meet these people; encouraged by what they do, encouraged by the conversations, encouraged because they allow me to stay with them (as I am this homeless wanderer around the planet) for two days, which is always kind.

That's just the way I function: I have to be mobile. I never found that standing in one place would bring the people for me; I have to be the one to go to *them,* so I go. And I mean that on a collaborative level: I'm always the one that seeks out the collaborators, that organizes the collaborations, that documents the collaborations, that finds a way to get it released. Because I have more energy, more stamina; I'm more stubborn, I'm more mobile—I don't know—because I'm not stuck in one place with all the restrictions that go with being tied to something like a house, a mortgage...

I do have apartments for the most part, usually, that I move to and abandon not long afterwards, but it's part of the nature of what I do. So I feel like I'm some kind of connective tissue that—if it doesn't bring people [physically] together—I am still sewing something connectively together, even if it's only a mutual inspirational instigation of thought. And that gives me great comfort to continue going on.

I'm not doing it for fifty, or one hundred, or two thousand (however many people might be in one given audience), I'm always doing what I do creatively for the few people that are on the guest list, and maybe the two others that have paid (!) that you know have some kind of desperate *hope* that they're going to hear one sentence—one paragraph—that is going to relieve them of something.

And that's very important to me. In that sense, having fluttered around many different movements or collaborators or cities or geographies, I feel that that's also part of my calling: to just be this cattle-prodder, this stimulator or this *appreciator*... because I'm very appreciative of what people do.

I thrive on the fact that other people are

creating within their own self-imposed exile
or in their own ghetto—and for *who,* we don't
know. We don't know who we're creating for,
but... actually, in a sense we *do* know who
we're creating for. Because we're creating for
some of our contemporaries... and for me, it's
also my forefathers.

I got so much strength, and stamina, and
stubbornness from Hubert Selby and the fact

Signing books for fans

that he lived for so long, basically undiscov-
ered... one of the greatest American novelists,
for who, fifteen years after the publication in
hardback of *Requiem for a Dream* in the U.K.,

the first printing sells out. Now, this is a horrible reality, but it gives me great encouragement because I know he was right. So, it's things like that...

I definitely have to take strength in a historical perspective, too. I have to take strength from the fact that Selby sold pornography for a couple of dollars a page. I have to take strength from the fact that when I met Hubert Selby, when he was sixty or whatever, he was an accountant.

▮ V: To pay the rent.

▮ LL: And he didn't have the ability to travel as I do, to go and encourage other people— even if they're just encouraged by the fact that I'm still out there stamping my feet and making a big hullabaloo wherever I go, and *laughing* in spite of it all.

What was interesting about that period, too (and it was the same on the West Coast), is that people brought a lot of their mixed formats to the scene. There were a lot of filmmakers and photographers and painters and visual artists and there were a lot of women doing film in New York, which was interesting: Vivienne Dick, and Beth and Scott B, and other people too, doing films. Film at that point (and

45

of course this is pre-digital, this is Super-8mm film): people would do films to be shown the next week, to be shown as soon as possible, like a document of their emotion at that time, or a political statement.

Beth and Scott B were very political about the films they made and they would be shown in the same clubs that people would perform in—it was just another *format,* another medium to get out the anxiety, the frustration, the horror, the nightmare that you felt at the time, so it was a perfect medium. Also what was wonderful (and what is still wonderful) about film is: you're using sound and vision and music and lighting and there is so much more going into a film, even if it's only you and Vivienne Dick with a camera... there's something very *intimate* about it, yet at the same time, you're bringing more elements to it.

I never felt like an actress, except for maybe in *Vortex* by Beth and Scott B I don't really feel like an actress. Those films led me on to Richard Kern, where I did films which were more autobiographical in nature and were more of a carry-on from Spoken Word. One thing that puts me into a very specific category of creation—which David Wojnarowicz fell into, Karen Finley to some part, and Wanda Coleman—for most of my creative output, I'm dealing with things that have affected me *personally*. I'm dealing with *real* stories from my experiences, and I think that's different from creating from fiction. So that kind of isolates you further in the outsider status; that kind of puts you in a marginalized area of creativity.

Those people certainly were not well-known at the time. They only became more well-known *in retrospect* because they had documentation that existed, they continued to show, and because at that time, places like the *Village Voice* had writers like J. Hoberman who were writing and interested in these topics, these themes, these filmmakers. There was more *support;* there was support for the scene on a larger scale—even if it's only from the *Village Voice* and the *New York Times*—but that was from *specific writers*.

▮ V: Who else besides J. Hoberman?

■ LL: Well, Robert Palmer, who'd often talk about the writings, or the films, or the music of that time, from the *New York Times*. Or C. Carr at the *Village Voice* who'd talk about

Performance Art.

■ V: I'm trying to put together the whole big picture, as much as possible, because it's always more complex than people think—

■ LL: I think what also helped at that time was: people were coming to music and music was kind of the *connector*... people were coming to music from paintings, or visual arts, or films, and collaborating together. I think part of what helped at the time were these loft parties, or the fact that there would be parties or events to go to where people could connect or mingle; there were clubs that people wanted to go to.

Now, people just don't like to leave their house. The big difference is: I don't want to go into a club unless they're paying me to walk into it, and most of the people I know are the same: they don't like the atmosphere of these places, the music is too loud, or you don't want to hear it... the atmosphere is not right. We weren't so picky in our early twenties; we just didn't want to be in our house because our house was surrounded by six feet of garbage on either side and smelled like death.

The more comfortable we get in our little

cocoons—that means I have to come to your table, and entertain you *here*...

One evening at the RE/Search office.
L to R: Marian Wallace, Lydia, Monte Cazazza, V. Vale

■ ■ ■

■ LYDIA LUNCH: According to your theory there was the Hippie movement, then the Punk movement, and those were only 10 years apart. Basically, before the Hippie movement the really important previous movements, which weren't as humongous, were the Surrealists and the Dadaists. Then we had to wait a good 30, 40, 50 years? So maybe now we're

coming up on the 30-year mark, and maybe
something is going to have to BE—and maybe
it *is* happening, and I hope not on the Internet.
Because I think the problem with *Internet*
communication is that there is *no emotional ex-change* involved. In order to gain from experience and to really appreciate true creativity,
you need a personal call-and-response, you
need an interchange, you need an exchange,
and preferably, you have to be breathing the
same air. You might not have to be exchanging
body fluids—but that might help, though!

And that's probably why it was so creative
and fertile, back in the mid- to late-seventies,
because everybody *was* exchanging fluids, and
the same air space. And we were sharing
everything—and contaminating and cross-pol-
linating—I think that's what causes this bee-
hive of creativity! If we're all in our separate
little cubicles, trying to exchange ideas—not
that that can't be stimulating, but I need to
smell it! And hence, to bring it back to myself
as I always will, I like to perform in an intimate setting. 'Cause I want people to be able
to smell it! I want to be able to see everyone's
eyes in the place. Hence the lateral nature of
my career, and the size of my audience, which

has not grown by one person in the past 28 years, which is fine by me, because I want to *give and receive* an intimate creative experience. And there is no commodification of that.

That's what was interesting about the mid- and late-seventies: things were very intimate because we were all crowded together, in a room not that much bigger than this, chewing the same atmosphere. I mean, I always feel I'm doing a one-on-one performance if there's one person, ten people, fifty or a hundred in an audience—that kind of defines what I do—it appears so conversational and intimate that way. But in the past, the intimacy was the fact that a lot of the same people would be at least in the same location, so other things could grow from that. Now, we're more spread out.

▌V: I haven't heard anyone talk about loft parties, but at least you could have conversations then. The music wasn't so loud.

■ LL: Exactly.

▌V: And there was a diversity.

■ LL: There was a diversity. It was bizarre because at a lot of the parties at that time, they wouldn't be playing the music that people were making, they would be playing more R&B, they would be playing groovier sounds, and the music would be more like lower volume and dance music, but I don't mean "dance music" the way we know it now. That was interesting, too.

Having no money forces you to be extra-creative... the only restraints are what people put upon themselves. I mean, that's it! Lack of budget has never *prevented* me from doing one single thing. You always find a way. You work with musicians in London, as I worked in Barcelona, in order to go to Istanbul, and that means: well, I'll have to sublet, I'll have to figure it out, I have to move around... That's the price that I pay, and it's a small price, compared to what I'm then able to accomplish. Because if I was tied to a mortgage, which I've *never* had; if I was tied to an apartment I can't give up because I have so much stuff I can't leave it; if I was tied to a location for whatever reason, I wouldn't be able to do... or maybe I *would!* Maybe I'd be *forced* to find a way to... But the nature of what I do is such that mobility is one of the most important things. Especially because where I'm hauled to is not always the same place. The calling shifts; sometimes it's Germany, Austria, Scandinavia that has a great demand for what I do; some-

LYDIA LUNCH

times it's France and Italy; sometimes I have
to find a place in-between; sometimes it's the
Midwest, sometimes it's the Mideast (I don't
mean the Middle East).

Because I demand that I support myself as
an artist (because I have no other skills!), part
of why I have to be mobile is to create and follow, create OR follow—I'm not sure—where
the trend of what I do can be placed to make
some financial gain: small as it may be; enough
to keep me going. So that's why I've had to live
in places like Pittsburgh for four years: because it was cheap, because I could afford it,
because then I had more time to create larger
things, like a larger body of photographic
work, sculptures, write a book.

For the same reasons, I moved to New Or-
leans: it was very cheap and I could develop
more of my photography, and work with more
people that maybe didn't come out of music,
but came out of photography. Part of it is,
that's my NATURE. I don't want to be tied to
one place, I don't want to be immobile. Part of
it is the nature of my work. I have to be that
way whether I like it or not. So I just go with
"the calling"; wherever I'm called to, that's
where I have to go, and I have to be able to do

53

it with a moment's notice and with not much but what I have on my back. You know, I do have possessions—I just can't move them with me! Because the most important things are not what I carry in my bag, but what I might get or give to whoever I'm going to be greeting at my next port of call—the next port of call of duty! Because that's going to be what *remains*. It's always been important (for me, at least) to be *in the face* of history. Because history is all over *me*, so I figure it's fair game to give it *back*.

What's interesting too is… with *you*, Vale, you've been in this one place for so long, it's like: *people come to you*. You've become an access/axis, of time, of geography, of history, of creativity. Because if you're steady enough in your place, then people are going to come to your table. And I'm the opposite; I'm like the equator circling the globe. That's kind of the interesting parallel between what we do. I'll run the marathon, and you'd rather sit here as it circles around you, snatching those important tidbits.

I'm always so used to mollycoddling, nurturing, encouraging, appreciating people… because that's how you get the gold! You don't get the gold by cutting their head off and throwing it down their throat—that's not gonna happen! At this point, I see *why* I'm able to work with so many people over and over again, because the bottom line is: *I* have to be the encourager! I'm not a mother; I have to mother! I have to nurture, I have to appreciate, I have to compliment, take note of the details. That's my job. I think it's very important, and I like doing it, because I *do* appreciate. Because as alone as I am, I'm *not*.

The basic bottom line of my moral ground (because that's what we're kind of looking for) is to *appreciate*. Because I'm perceived to be so negative, so angry, so harsh ("the Queen of Harsh," as I've been tagged); because people are so frightened, in general, of an aggressive, articulate, intelligent, sexual woman... still, in this year 2005; because my reputation precedes me, which has only to do with the "fictionalizing" of certain elements of my personality that whoever, for whatever reason, cares to create (my image, my reputation). It's always very important to me to be as encouraging as possible to everyone that I come in contact with! And that's something that people don't really know about: *how I truly am.* The only reason I'm able to work with all these different collaborators is because: first and foremost, I want to *encourage* what they do, I want to encourage them to create something that wouldn't exist without this marriage happening.

■

Look, I may be one of the most prolific people I know but I'm also one of the laziest! It's either one or the other. There's nothing I love more than lying in bed, doing *nothing*. Not even reading. There's nothing I love more than just floating on a sea of bed. I love to float in bed; I love to disappear into bed. I love it. Because if I'm not doing that... I'm running maniacally on to the next project!

I'm sure most of my stamina is just attitude! Again, back to stubbornness: I'm not going to get beaten down, they're not going to stymie my energy; I'm just not going to be stopped; they can't steal my utopia! They can't steal it; they can't steal my pleasure. That's basically the ultimate rebellion—it always comes back to that. No matter how horrible it is, and how horrible they pretend it to be, and how much fear they monger, I'm not going to be frightened, and have to somehow live outside of it—while still commenting on it! I'm not going to get their cancer, it's just down to that. I'm not going to get their cancer; I'm not going to get their moral pollution, their emotional pollution; I'm not going to get corrupted by it. It's like—I've cleansed my soul.

◼ V: How do you plan and organize?

◼ LL: It's not like I'm so driven that I've got the next five years [figured out]. I mean, I have to be disciplined enough to know what I'm

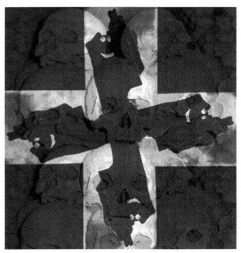

"My AMERIKKKA" by Lydia Lunch

doing six months down the line, just to keep from being completely economically destitute. I live a borderline existence, but then I don't have expensive habits... but moving a lot is expensive! Even if you're not taking much with you, it becomes an expensive habit. And it's risky, because you're going to a country—I never get help from the country I'm in, necessarily—it's not like I count on any one place to support me in any way; I have to be very independent. But I still have to know what's going on at least six months down the road, so that I don't fall into complete financial [chaos]; be completely bankrupt! Which I've been... and I don't mean just bankrupt that I'm in credit card debt, I mean: *no money at all*. It's a risk when you work on this level. Sometimes you become homeless and you just have to count on your benefactors. And they're not many, because who can afford to take you in?

So you have to be cautious, you have to be very disciplined about that. It's not as if I'm planning so much... You know, I just create at the pace at which it's like breathing. Because I create in so many different formats, just one thing flows into the other. You know, I'm working on photography, I'm working on installations, I'm working on music, I'm doing Spoken Word—and Spoken Word is ultimately what always ends up supporting me anyway! Because there's no budget involved. You can do a few Spoken Word shows and you're immediately out of the poor house. That helps! At least it keeps you afloat as you run amok—run rampant—from one end of the globe to the other.

∎ V: You've given me a thought: "Utopia" as not a noun but a VERB—and it sounds like you're already kind of in a utopia?

∎ LL: Well, exactly, because there's absolutely no restrictions on… I don't consider that I'm financially restricted by anything, especially living in Europe now—flights are so cheap everywhere: you can fly to London from Barcelona for 15 bucks. Yeah, 30 dollars return [round trip], if you plan it a few weeks in advance. So you're not even stymied by that anymore. Because I am allowed—because I *insist* on being so free—there's nothing hanging over my head. Therefore, what could be a better feeling than knowing that: You know what? You don't like this, you don't like that, you're fickle, you're bored, you wanna see—you just GO! I mean, there's no restrictions on what I do. Again, the discipline of the six months down the line of knowing which shows, knowing what I have to do, just to be able to... stay *under* the radar, I guess...

▮ V: Keep your head above water—

■ LL: Keep my head; keep doggy-paddling; the crabwalk sideways through my career, as I call it—that's just *bliss!* I want for nothing. Nothing is hanging over my head, I do what I want, with who I want, wherever I want... I mean, what the hell! I'd be sick if I wasn't happy...

▮ V: What *is* an installation?

■ LL: I did an installation this year called "You Are Not Safe In Your Own Home." It was based on a Spoken Word piece I had called "Memory and Madness," which was about the disintegration of an abusive, drug-addled relationship, and the psychology and emotion inherent in that. I wanted to do a physical representation of that, so that I could involve photography, lighting, music, sound, home porno, telephone stalking, and all the elements... in order to force someone, *environmentally*, to be contaminated by the end result of this experience. So instead of just giving a Spoken Word show, they're forced into the environment—that's how I view an installation.

I mean, when I do an installation, it's like you're going into a world. Fortunately for you, you can go in for a few minutes, and then step out, and leave. But this is *The Hell*. This is the contaminated remains of the end result of an over-stimulated relationship. That's what that was about. You can see the photos on my web-site: "You Are Not Safe In Your Own Home."

But I used actual home-porno of the guilty party and myself. You see, once again, it has to be that intimate. I did reframe it so that I cut his head off, though. So he became, there-fore, "any man." It was a natural progression from what I do in Spoken Word, I thought, and I really enjoyed it because it allows me to bring a more visual sense, even if the visuals are a destroyed room. It allows me to impreg-nate further, and contaminate, with a more in-timate experience than just the sound of my voice. Which can be very intimate!

That's what *my* installations are about; I don't know about anyone else's.

▮ V: You and J.G. Ballard said that the porno film is the true future of film.

■ LL: Well [sigh], again, like drugs, we need *more* porno, not less. The problem with porno is that it's all so much *alike*. I think we need

61

many new *alternative* kinds of pornography. Actually, now there are many kinds of pornography compared to in the seventies, or even the eighties, when pornography was in very few hands, by very few people, all of a certain type: middle-aged or older white men. And I think that has changed considerably. I guess if you want to reduce it to basics... it would be kind of sad if that was the end result of all film... just simply pornography. It's just not *enough*.

▮ V: I think J.G. Ballard meant: Imagine making a film about what a truly real relationship *is,* between a *real* couple. If you wanted to take it that far, would it also include authentic lovemaking?

■ LL: I did use authentic home video—without the person's knowledge—in this installation, because he was the guilty party who inspired this installation. So, that's kind of beyond bootlegging. But again, he was saved by having his head cut off. I just do what comes natural to me—I guess because I'm less inhibited, or I don't feel that anything is a taboo. So I don't feel that I'm breaking taboos by using my own pornography in my installation. I mean... I've told everything I possibly could about the most intimate details of my life. Because I know that I'm not alone in going through these. So it's the universal nature of these traumas that is *important* for me to delve into.

■ V: Well, all art—I hate to use such a self-conscious word as "archetype"—but I think the art you connect with has kind of deeper, more universal resonances.

■ LL: Exactly. It has to go as deep as possible; it has to be as intimate as possible. Maybe because that's the art that impacts *me* the most. The art that impacted me the most was the most intimate, therefore that's what I have to give back. I feel that especially from a feminine perspective, there just isn't enough extreme intimate material out there! It always has to be romanticized, or glamorized, or cosseted, or coy, or hidden—it just never cuts to the bone deeply enough. Whereas men are allowed to be as revelatory as they want to be, as harsh, as pornographic, as extreme, as real, as intimate... it's a given.

■ V: You're talking, really, about expressing more "truth?" That word?

■ LL: That's all I'm dealing with.

■ V: Truth and Beauty.

■ LL: Well, you flatter me. Let's not flirt, please.

▮ V: No; more universal—

■ LL: [laughs] I *know* what you're talking about. Yeah, yeah, yeah.

▮ V: Well, that's what art's about! I mean, do you think "beauty" is a forbidden word? No one uses that word.

■ LL: No, I don't think it's forbidden, absolutely not. No, no. But it's not what *I* focus on. Because, especially coming from a female point of view, I don't feel it's necessary for *me* to play upon beauty. I'm looking to turn the horror, the ugliness, the brutality, into a positive experience—whether or not that's beautiful. I don't use language *beautifully*, I want to use language *seductively*. But it's not for me (especially as a woman) to beautify *anything*. I mean, *I want people to see the beauty in what I do, in spite of the horror of what I present.* That simple. Good luck!

▮ V: Thank you, Lydia Lunch.

■■■

With members of 2009 Teenage Jesus: Jim Sclavunos, Al Kizys. Note torn drum case bottom right.

On the RESURRECTION OF TEENAGE JESUS

After her Teenage Jesus and the Jerks show in San Francisco, Lydia returns for another taping of *The Counter Culture Hour* with host V. Vale.

■ LYDIA LUNCH: All of what I do has always been word-based. But the thought struck that I had to do something—use another *tool-weapon,* if you will—to promote what the words *were,* and hence, I created the sound of Teenage Jesus.

I had to find the drummer at the time—who refused me for six months—I insisted I would teach him how to play drums, not that *I* knew how, but I knew how it had to sound. Then we went through a series of bass players. In creating the music, I wanted something that expressed—musically and rhythmically—the hatred, anger, and vile poisonous nature of my personal beast. And it was just very automatic that this music basically wrote itself.

I came with no musical knowledge, but wanted something that broke from traditional music... and also broke from the music that inspired me, like Richard Hell and The Voidoids or Patti Smith, who to me were far too TRADITIONAL. I needed something that ANNIHILATED MELODY, eliminated "normal" structure, and was like a jack hammer to the inner eardrum.

There's two important elements to Teenage Jesus: the precision of the rhythm, and the brutarian nature of a slide guitar which is equivalent to a piano wire inserted into your ear! And that has to do with the type of guitar: a Fender, and the type of amp: a Fender Twin Reverb (which is the only amp because it's tube-based). It's the only guitar

and amp that, together, make this piercing ca-
cophony of BEAUTIFUL DISHARMONY.

Don't ask—I don't know, it just happened.
Think of a title, write the music. One song is
called "Freudian Flop"—it's thirty seconds
long—don't ask me what it means or what it's
about! I think maybe the first song I wrote was
called "Red Alert": "*Na-na-na-na-na-na-na,
na-na-na-na-na-na-na*"—like a red alert, like
a fire alarm, like a warning.

▌ V: "No Wave" inspired a wave of creativity
in you that transcends limitations—

■ LL: It's just that small path that I continue
to cross, and the need to spread the viral in-
fection of my creative process. What's interesting now is that we're back full circle—I call
it the "retro-virus." We're back, and initially
this concept was re-instigated by Thurston
Moore [Sonic Youth] a year ago, when he put
out what I call the "Love Letter to Lydia
Lunch's No Wave Encyclopedia" with Byron
Coley, this book covering the No Wave period
in New York [*No Wave: Post-Punk. Underground. New York. 1976–1980*]. And he sug-
gested that there be a Teenage Jesus revival,
knowing I've never done a revival. Look, I'm
going forward, my trajectory is *this* (or should

I say, the crabwalk of my career, sideways). I said, "Well, they're almost all dead—who's playing bass: you?" And he said, "Yes!"

So, Thurston Moore consented to play the bass, to have a Teenage Jesus reunion a year ago, June, in New York, to celebrate an exhibition and the release of his *No Wave* book. So, it was Jim Sclavunos (who was the original bass player) but now on *drum,* and Thurston Moore on bass. We did two shows in New York at the Knitting Factory, June of last year, and then we did two shows at All Tomorrow's Parties festival in the U.K.

You know, for years these *documentaries* have been coming out—I just called this the "retro-virus." So many people are interested now, and these documentaries, I mean—I'm *done* with it, although I know I'm an important part of it. Thurston is a completist, so this book is good. So I'm like: reunion, revival, retro, nostalgic?!

But when you get back to reality, to me the responsibility is this: there are so few women... There *are* a lot of women doing avant-garde or intense or interesting music—maybe not as many as there were in the late seventies... but there's really few women doing very ugly, uncompromised, brutarian, fascist beats—maybe there's only ONE. Therefore, as a *responsibility,* especially because there's a lot of young girls in the audience (the first band, T.I.T.S., is definitely inspired by my style of guitar playing; there's a few others inspired by the No Wave)—well, I WANT to be inspirational to *people that want to make uncompromising art.*

To me it's ridiculous—it's more Dada *now* than it ever was. That's part of the charm of Teenage Jesus: its completely Dadaist routine. It's ridiculous in the extreme, it's brutarian, it's vulgar and it's f—kin' fun. So, in the day of overproduced pop-porn, disco bulls—t which promotes an ideal of beauty that no one can live up to, and an expensive production that no one should *aspire* to, it makes sense for a random scattering of shows to bring back the nightmare of oral terror that is Teenage Jesus. That's why I'm here, or was here ... and it's the last show, so I'm glad you saw it.

I'm not consigning it forever. I mean, if there's a special reason... but, *this is it.* We did five shows in the States; we did four shows last year. You know, San Francisco was important in that period of music, so we wanted to come back to the people that are still alive carrying on the tradition that we all started back then: the tradition of making Outsider Music and Art... and then also for this new generation of kids who are doing great stuff and are really exciting. The second band, Burmese, was also great—I mean, they were more influenced by the Second Wave in a sense, like the Swans—but they were also influenced a bit by Teenage Jesus and the stop-start rhythm. So *good times*.... with horrible sounds!

▮ V: Stop-and-start noise-guitars, thunderous bass, shrieking vocals—

■ LL: I don't know the effect it has on the audience, I only know that the original intention was to bring the INNER TANTRUM of my diseased psyche to the forefront of the stage. Because it is like a baby screaming. The guitar is like a hysterical baby screaming, the words are very infantile—there's one called "Baby Doll," "Orphans"—I mean, these are very infantile emotions, the best line, of course, being, "I can't talk/ I can't enunciate/ And I'm treated like Sharon Tate" from a song called "The Closet." "I woke up dreaming/ I woke up screaming/ I woke up heaving/ I woke up bleeding": it's very primal, infantile, teenage—

it should be PRE-teenage, tantrum-izing. It is the tantrum scream of a tortured, teenage terrorist... in a nutshell.

■ V: What's great are the stop-and-starts—

■ LL: It was so important to be tight, even in the day. I mean, we rehearsed endlessly. Because, if you're going to be that minimal, it has to be PRECISE. My favorite line is, "If you're gonna be this ugly, you've gotta be tight." It's gotta be tight, otherwise it's just noise.

There is a noise element, but that's not the building block of it. The building block of it is a PRECISION EXORCISM: taking a tantrum—which is an uncontrollable outpouring of rage and anxiety—and finessing it into mechanized abuse. In a sense, turning the abuse back around. It's like a beating: if you're being beaten, as opposed to being *whaled* upon. Well, a fight is sloppy, a beating [makes repetitive hitting sound] is very precise.

So, perhaps incorporating the chaos of the abuse that I felt at the hands of not only my family but of the world in general, and then reconfiguring it into a *precise battery* to then dish back into the face of the rest of the planet... again, this music makes me very CALM.

A RE/Search Pocketbook

Onstage, I'm in a dead calm for this. It's very automatic without it being mechanical. But… how can it be automatic when I've done now, nine shows after thirty years of *not* doing it?! There's something about it that's so true to Who I Am, in a sense, maybe because it was the first act of creation. There's something that's so perfectly in sync with a part of me that needs release, that it becomes the most calming performance of my entire career; it becomes something that's in sync with what needs to come out of me. And the dead stare, which is what I had originally because it was so anti-audience, or anti-participatory, or anti-communal—it was an affront against ANY community. It didn't want fans, it didn't want an audience, it did not have a mosh pit… there were twenty people at the show, not two hundred.

▮ V: There are stark silences in the set—

■ LL: So, a calm comes over me—I guess it's like a *killer calm*. Like the calm a killer might have… right before they turn the gas on. It's the most comfortable thing for me to do; it's more comfortable than any other form of music. It feels the most right. Maybe because it is singularly my path. That music, Teenage

Jesus specifically, is a singular-direction path that so perfectly defines a part of what I need to express.

And *beautiful* last night when the drum— the singular drum—[broke]. In the original ten-minute sets back in '77, the drummer

Bradley Field would almost always break a snare drum within ten minutes. When you only have that to focus everything on, you're beating the s—t out of it. When Sclavunos broke his drum, he refused to replace it with another snare (not that he has another one of these *deep* ones), but instead went back to the origins of how music was made and beat on the box—

▌V: The drum case—

■ LL: The drum case. Sticks flying like chopsticks, rocks against each other—*yeah,* banging two rocks against each other. And because the rhythms are so basic and so driving and so... *seductive* in a sense, it's then coupled with this horrendous, tight, yet still improvised to some degree, *noise.* The noise is justified by the return of the precise rhythm. It always ends completely precisely. And to complement or INSULT each other, we have the two extremes which connect.

So, that's one form that the music takes: the brutarian, pounding, driving, precise rhythm, followed by a structured burst of semi-improvised chaos, returning again to the beat.

Then we have the hyper-fast followed by the HYPER-NIGHTMARE, which are the

SLOW SONGS… which are really a hypnotic narcosis, and mainly about the nightmare— *nightmares,* specifically—but also the nightmare of existence.

So if one song is called "I Woke Up Dreaming"—and the slow is the most hypnotic—or "The Closet" (claustrophobic nightmare), we have the two extremes: from "Red Alert" (the warning signal *"na-na-na-na,"* "Freudian Flop" *"ne-ne-ne-ne-ne"*… to *"dooong-doong"* like the funeral bell *"dooong-doong"*; *"la-la-la-la"* becomes a nursery rhyme: *"la-la-la-la, booong, doong-doong"*). So, between the TANTRUM and the FUNERAL MARCH: that's the trajectory this music takes, and there's no room for any other kind of sound or speed or pace. It's a slug across a razor blade, or it's an ambulance racing down the street: these are the extremes of the reality that this tantrum-izing teenage terrorist inhabits… again, at the EXTREMES OF EMOTIONS.

■ V: How can the band be so "tight"?

■ LL: They fear the coat hanger, what can I say—they're trained by the coat hanger! Mistakes are not greeted gently. And, also, it becomes a running joke, because if I do not like the way a song sounded, then we will do it again. If there was one or two notes I did not like, we will do it again—it doesn't matter *who* made them. If the song was too perfect, we will do it again just to get it again to that point. So they're always on the edge of the stage because they don't know what might come next: again, or abort [laughs].

▮ V: Some have said your music has fascist rhythms—

■ LL: It's using a fascist rhythm as a complaint against fascism. Again, it's like in my political speeches: using the language or the statistics of the enemy. Using an aggressive, macho stance to complain against an aggressive, macho stance as part of my *contrarian spin-around.* So, that's just part of the perversity of the creature that I am: EMBODYING, in a sense THE ENEMY... BECOMING THE BULLY to make a point *against* the bully. Because I am a bully, but ultimately, I'm *not* a bully. I'm cattle-prodding, encouraging... but I AM a bully, and the bully is both what I despise and admire in myself. And it's using what, ultimately, you hate the most.

And the same with a fascist rhythm: to complain against the fascism of everyday life I use, in a sense—not that it's the music of fascism, but it's a music that is somehow linked to what you would *imagine* it to be... One of the jokes that we made when Teenage Jesus was first happening was, "If they played this music in factories, workers would work a lot faster and harder, just to get the hell out!" [repeated thumping to a beat] That's the sound of Going to War, that's the sound of the guitar *goose-stepping.* I used to use a beer bottle, or a knife, but now I use a glass slide; I don't use a steel slide.

▮ V: Professionally crafted?

▮ LL: Yeah, just a normal glass slide. Back in the day it could be a beer bottle, it could be a knife—it didn't matter. But the glass slide is preferable.

I think that I'm one of the best guitar players, too, but that's in MY universe—there's not many; there's one: ME [laughs]. I mean, obviously, in other universes I love Paul Leary of the Butthole Surfers, Rowland S. Howard, Robert Cline... I love a million guitar players. But again, in my own world there's not many of us doing that.

Nels Cline: when I was doing a retrospective—with Nels Cline, Algis Kizys, Vinnie Signorelli who was in the Swans, and Norman

Westberg who was also in the Swans—we tried to cover "Orphans" and Nels Cline couldn't play it right. This is a master guitar player and I'm like, "It sounds like s—t" because there was one tiny (and I couldn't even explain it or show him)—there was one tiny, off-rhythmic beat he wasn't nailing: ONE. And, of course you can't teach someone—I mean they can *try* to imitate that slide, but it really must pour out of the bloodstream.

▪ V: Initially, what was your theory?

■ LL: There *was* no theory involved. Somebody gave me a broken guitar that was almost as big as a bass, that I think had three strings, and that's how I wrote most of the songs, other than the slide parts, of course... It's how I wrote the rhythm. I don't know a chord at all, I don't know a single chord. I'm tone deaf, in a sense. I mean, I can't sing scales. I know how to tune the guitar with a tuner—that's not the issue.

This is not about chords, it's about getting the appropriate sound to back up, especially, the *lyrics*... or to further the climb with complete disharmony. The music has to be disharmonious but in a very specific way. It's gotta have a *just-so-awful* sound. I mean, it's very important that the guitar is in tune—strange, I know, but it's true. There's no special tuning here.

I used a "box" [effect] only on one song, and only because the Fender Twin Reverb amps—tube amps—are not as perfect as they were in the late seventies. So for one song, which I really need a long slide on—it's the only concession to modern technology—I have to use a box on ONE SONG which has the longest slide, which I WAS very much against... With the amps today, even if they're older amps, you can't get the sound of a tube amp from that period—it's just impossible. So the only concession is a "Screaming Bird" (it's called) box for one song... the rest is just amp and guitar sound. But Algis Kizys, on bass, is just a thunder machine anyway. I mean, to me this has the perfect sound of how the band should be.

Originally, the bass players were—the first one, Reck, was a Japanese guitar player that we took down to bass—he was *too musical.* The next one, Gordon Stevenson, knew nothing and couldn't even hold his bass well. Then Jim Sclavunos came in, and Sclavunos was a very good bass player at that time and musical enough, but thunderous. I think Algis has the power of the thunder to give complement to the brittleness of the guitar.

I think with this balance, it's a very good blend of the instruments… just to have that most heinous cry to complement the vocal line, the words…

It's not how my theory is based—on Major or Minor—it's based on the most effective placement of my fingers to make the most PERFECTLY HORRIBLE SOUND for *that second*—that's it, wherever that might be. That was the most difficult thing to figure out when I came back to redo the songs.

All the slide parts came back to me instantaneously. Someone would tune my guitar maybe once a month and it would come to have a certain disharmony—it was still a normal tuning, but out of tune *naturally*. And to figure out where the rhythm was being played was quite difficult, because the rhythm came back to me, but since I don't know where the chords are—*where* am I actually playing the chords?! That was the most difficult thing to figure out about this.

You can't reproduce a disharmonic tuning because you're three weeks into a four-week run of rehearsing. That was most difficult for whoever was playing bass (Al, or Thurston when he was playing the bass, in these latest shows). The bass was *basically* in tune, but I can't tell them HOW to complement what I'm doing RHYTHMICALLY IN TIME to my so-called "chord."

So... I have two albums coming out. Big Sexy Noise is my hard rock band. Because

Big Sexy Noise

after thirty years of political dissent and after so many years of the Bush family regime, saying as much about politics as I can, I felt it was just time to ROCK and kick out the mother-f—kin' jams! And it's not because the "beige puppet" is in office (Barack Obama—I don't have much hope in him either)… however, it's time to f—kin' *rock*.

So, next week Big Sexy Noise—which includes Terry Edwards and James Johnston and Ian White—we have a Hard Rock album coming out and we go on tour in Europe and we put out a six-track vinyl in the summer, so there's a full album coming out.

Then I have an album with Cypress Grove which is what I call the "Sunday Country Record"—it doesn't have a title yet but it's kind of channeling the inner Bobbie Gentry. That album came out of a project Cypress Grove had proposed to me because he had worked with Jeffrey Lee Pierce of Gun Club, right before Jeffrey died, doing the "Ramblin' Jeffrey Lee" project.

There's a tribute to Jeffrey Lee's music *pre-*Gun Club that comes out next month with Nick Cave, Mark Lanegan, Debbie Harry… I'm on it and while I did the two songs of Jeffrey Lee's early material, Cypress Grove and I just continued working.

Once the tribute record comes out, we'll put our record out probably early next year. It's very exciting to me because it's more traditional in a sense, but I think it occupies a realm of music of which—it's hard to find something that's SEDUCTIVE, not corny; mellow but INTERESTING. You can't define the genre because it's not Country, it's not Blues, it's not bar—it's just… inventing, again, another genre that once again suits the words which suit the vocals.

I'm at the point with my voice where I could do something like this, because previously I had such a reticence to singing. I mean, this was the problem with 8-Eyed Spy: they wanted me to *sing,* and I didn't want to *sing.* I mean, I was anti-singing… it was not the POINT for me to VOCALIZE. The point for me to vocalize was to get the emotion and the words out… that didn't mean melody, necessarily.

Not that I haven't sung and not that there weren't musical elements to "Shotgun Wedding" and various other things I've done. But now, at this point, to even *contraire* myself—I shall sing! And what better time—while the retro-virus of Teenage Jesus is happening—than to do a "Sunday Country Record" and a Rock record?! So, I mean we've always got these balls flying in the air at all times. As you know, that's how I function… the UNHOLY

TRINITY. Just three of my inner bitches, coming out at once to play!

■ V: Talk about your slide guitar "technique"—

■ LL: Even *I'm* not anticipating where the slide might go, but I know when it will begin and when it will stop. A certain amount of "improv" now in this music was important to me. Because yes, I can play "Orphans" exactly like the record! But without a certain amount—because to me, I'm sure that there might be a time in the not-too-distant future where you see me doing a band of improv with guitar and maybe two guitars and maybe two drums, because I do love to play the guitar!

I mean, I play it on some of the new Cypress Grove stuff—a very different STYLE of guitar—a slide guitar, but a very different style. But, I love to play improv guitar. I had improv groups with, for instance, Connie Burg and Pat Place. We've done shows together. Three slide guitar players in New York, the three women slide guitar players from that period—fantastic!

Connie Burg and I did an album which was the soundtrack to *The Right Side of My Brain* [film directed by Richard Kern] of instrumental music, mostly just playing in rehearsal and recording, not live.

The guitar may be back out of the closet for a while now, in a different incarnation, coming soon. I have been playing with this three-piece group in Barcelona called Les Aus and it's synth, drums and I play guitar. I've done a few shows with this group and that's quite beautiful... we went to the Lausanne Film Festival and did a few shows in Barcelona.

But as far as improv in *this country* [U.S.] on my guitar, there's no call for it. It's something I will do in Europe, but there's no call for me here—for any of this, anyway. I mean, I'm here to milk the bank on these shows—to add to the economic collapse of this country. It's one of the reasons I came back: to let me help you lose more money! I'm good at it...

■ V: How do you deal with the economics of a band touring—

■ LL: I pay them [band members] in advance so they can deposit it before I hit the road. Why should I carry their money—not that I'm going to lose it, but I don't want to be responsible for that. Pay 'em; they're not going anywhere. *I'm* much happier to get paid in advance, like, "Thanks! Don't have to worry about THAT."

I've worked with the same booking agents and the same clubs for many years. Look, a lot of these shows—five in the States—they all KNEW they would lose money. They knew it; I mean it's pre-determined they will have to lose some money because I do have expenses—it's not like I'm asking so much, but I have a band to pay, we are flying, I'm coming all the way from Europe, and we know the audience—I mean, there were what? Two hundred and fifty people at the most there last night? There's no more; that's the audience, unless it's at All Tomorrow's Parties or a big festival where it's ten times the original audience. What do you want?!

I don't think there is an issue to try to rip me off, because I've never dealt with major labels or big booking agencies. I deal with a lot of the same clubs and when it's time for them to lose the money, I've got my motto which is: "I've got one night to make it, you have three hundred and sixty-four to make up what you lose! What are you gonna do?" They can't barter with that.

I mean, if it comes to it, there is physical violence—I will not hold back. If I need to commit an act of physical violence to get paid, I will do it. Now, usually the THREAT is enough. But I haven't had to threaten anyone in about fifteen years. If I tell someone, "I will stab you unless you pay me," they are going to believe me, because I might just do it—I might NOT, but don't make me! But it doesn't resort to that. And I think that, you know, fortunately with this much time under my bridge, there is a certain amount of RESPECT. I don't wanna work with places that don't have it...

You know, working with someone like Dawn Holliday [booker at Slim's, San Francisco] is great. She's put on so many of my Spoken Word events. She knows what the situation is, and she's happy to support something like this—I'm not fraternizing with the enemy. So, who's gonna rip me off—my friends? I don't think so.

I think that by nature, more people will stay away from me because they know they won't be able to get at me. So, it's more about inviting people into my life who I want there. Because they might already have the fear factor, they might not know how I really am. Because it's still so unusual to see a woman who's aggressive, not full of s—t, blunt, and speaks her f—kin' mind… That, right there, is a nightmare that most people don't want to challenge… until they talk to me for two minutes and realize, "What is to fear?" *I* am not the enemy, I am the all-inclusive community organizer: "Welcome!"

I'm doing multi-media shows at museums with my video backdrops based on my photography, usually using a back-up singer who's translating a quarter of the text into French or Spanish. That's at museums, with psycho-ambient music I've created.

▮ V: Psycho-ambient? I've never heard that word before.

■ LL: It's what I do. So, I have a show called "Ghosts of Spain," and "Amnesia." It's just video backdrops that I've created, with psycho-ambient music… a lot about amnesia, relationships, ghosts, abandoned spaces, hauntings… and this is what I bring to the museums. As we stand within the giant ruins of, for instance, Belchite [Zaragoza, Spain], the ghost town I'm obsessed with… and then use another female presence onstage, in another language, to bring another essence to the words… very beautiful performances. That's what I can do in Europe because there are places like museums where they should have things like this. So that's one place my photography is going.

I have to live in Europe at this point. Europe has supported me for more than a decade, anyway. Why should I live on the West Coast—or even the East Coast—and have to fly to have the opportunities I need to have in order to be able to support myself—which is not an easy job.

I struggle. I have to be very organized. I have to be very disciplined. I have to be very far-forward thinking in order to survive on a day-to-day basis without a day job—which I've never held in my adult life, and which I refuse to ever have!

It's impossible at this point: what would I *do?* So, then I become the artistic juggler and I have to be organized, disciplined, and focused on what's gonna happen next year and that becomes a habit trail all on its own. It's like the PRISON OF FREEDOM, because you don't have a day job… but that means you are still tied to an economic reality…

It seems to be a very liberated lifestyle, but you still have to have incredible discipline and be thinking a year in advance sometimes. It's the PRISON OF LIBERATION, it's the prison of being free from the nine-to-five. It's still a prison to some degree, because I'm doing it all myself—I mean, I have a booking agent, but that's IT. I have to be out there hunting, inventing new projects, finding a new area, mining a different type of venue… It's still a lot of work, but it's work that is a duty, that must be done, that is a calling, and that I wish I could say keeps me sane, but that's not the issue. The issue is to EXPRESS MY INSANITY, to *externalize* it, so it doesn't pollute me further, because obviously, I'm the healthiest woman you know!

The following interview/conversation excerpts are from a few visits and a phone call, all in the 21st century.

BARCELONA

▮ VALE: So, Lydia, Vale here. I assume you're in Barcelona?

■ LYDIA: Yes! Don't you wish you were here?

▮ V: Of course! Are you kidding?!

■ LL: I wish you were, too.

▮ V: You lucky girl—what good karma! You're in paradise—you can go out at 2 a.m. and sit outside and have dinner. That's amazing.

■ LL: Exactly… and just all the types of performance I can do here! It's the privilege of being able to perform in so many different kinds of circumstances.

I have not been healthier in my adult life than since living for almost eight years in Spain. I know where all my vegetables come from. Monsanto [agricultural-biotechnology group infamous for genetically-engineered foods] has been banned from quite a few places. People in Europe are not buying it! Healthiest I've been in my life: living in Spain. You just know it, you feel it. The food, I mean. Whereas it's disgusting *here* [U.S.].

▮ MARIAN WALLACE: Was it hard to move to Europe?

■ LL: Are you kidding? [laughs] Hard to move?! I sold *everything* and left—easy!

▮ MW: And you're not trying to get a job there, so they don't say, "No, you can't have one."

■ LL: Well, I work a lot more there than I can here!

■ MW: But it's your own entrepreneurship....

■ LL: I can't do what I do in *this* country.

■ MW: But you aren't taking a Spanish job away; you're doing your own—

■ LL: Job?! Why are you swearing at me?! How dare you insult me! Are you condemning me to work?! I wish I had *one* f—king job instead of *ten*—

■ V: —or 20!

■ LL: How much easier my life would be. Certainly, it's not boring!

YOU could *easily* have such a nice life. You're silly. Why? Why, when you know so much, do you live here in the U.S.? Why, smart as you are, are you not running a museum somewhere? Are you here to go down with the ship? Are you here

Marian Wallace, Lydia Lunch

to the bitter end, my friends? Are you silly? Have you been brain-damaged by the food, the water, the air, the politics? Whatever.

■ MW: Well, California is not as bad as some places—

▌V: —San Francisco, specifically.

■ LL: Yeah, of course, because you'll be the first to fall into the ocean! Because this is the first place where all the nuclear radiation from Japan will wash up. So, I guess, it's not that bad: you'll be the first to go! Good idea!

▌V: At least we're on a hill—

■ LL: Sure, good! Your reasons for living here are so flimsy I couldn't write my name on the piece of paper they're printed on. *Whatever*. If you get a dinghy and you decide to sail...[singing] "Fukushima, Fukushima"—it's coming. Maybe the Pacific Garbage Dump will absorb all of Fukushima [2011 Japanese nuclear disaster site] like a giant maw.

▌V: It's like "Fujiyama Mama" [1957] by what's her name? She's a living legend—not Loretta Lynn but—

■ LL: Not Wanda Jackson?

▌V: It WAS Wanda Jackson! "Fukushima Mama" instead of "Fujiyama Mama"—

■ LL: I just picked it out of my hair... Anyway, we're all still alive.

A RE/Search Pocketbook

■ V: [laughs] So far!
■ LL: Not bad, not bad.

BIG SISTER

■ LL: I was thinking about you today because I
have to write a few sentences for this performance in Washington, D.C. I've been doing occa-
sional performances with this avant-garde
violinist, Mia Zabelka. She was invited to this
Sonic Circuit Festival in Washington, D.C. And
I really didn't wanna go because I don't like to
come to the States—I don't like to travel that far.
So, I told her a ridiculous fee… and she came up
with it!

In the meantime, I have another show in
Barcelona that's very important—I *have* to do it.
So just yesterday I told her, "Well…Washington,
D.C.: Surveillance State, Patriot Act; I could send
you a VIRTUAL performance." I would be "Big
Sister," with my big mouth and face live behind
her, for some of the pieces she would play. Yeah,
BIG SISTER'S COMIN'! So, yeah, I will be per-
forming on video. It will be like *1984* but I'll be
giving it *back* to them!
■ V: Wow—that's a great idea—

■ LL: Yeah, isn't it? Not to have to take the flight, and deal with all the above-mentioned. I'm just writing up the concept today, so I was thinking about you. I'm like, "I'm glad I'm going to be speaking to Vale—he is going to love this idea!" My big mouth, just giant-sized, giving back to Washington, D.C. everything they've given to us—

▮ V: Yeah, *you're* the one who, *ages* ago—

■ LL: —got away! I'm the refugee. I'm in self-imposed exile, honey—

▮ V: As they say, "Nice work if you can get it!"

■ LL: Yeah! Well, certainly I get a lot more work *here* than I can in America, so there ya go! Sure, *we all* can get more work here, you know? It must be bleak on that side of the ocean AND on that side of the country.

I'm really sorry you're living in these times in that place. I mean, you *have* to, as an "Archivist of Culture" and a "Historian of Hysteria," but better you than me! I did my time! And I feel like I'm one of the original whistleblowers. That's what I'm gonna put in this little press release: "I've been blowing the whistle since before I could speak!"

▮ V: That's a really great line. Like, "Blowing the whistle on war crimes should not be a crime"— that's on this Bradley Manning poster I have up.

■ LL: It's just outrageous. I'm gonna send to you MANDATORY reading—the *Washington Post* did a two-year investigation on how many people are employed by spy agencies in the United States. It was a ten-part series and it was *absolutely* horrifyingly shocking. I just pulled it up today, because I was so excited by my new concept of "BIG SISTER, The No Wave Nostradamus."

▮ V: Sixty years after "Big Brother" was thought of (because Orwell's book came out in 1949), finally someone comes up with "Big Sister." Hey, there's still work to be done!

■ LL: Isn't there?! Oh my Christ! And, you know, the work to be done, for me, is *here.* [in Barcelona, Spain]

Soon I'll be on the next tour—*somebody's* got to be out there protesting!

BALLARDIAN

■ LL: I hope to be your next J.G. Ballard—

▮ V: That's a brilliant idea. I was thinking only of men—

■ LL: *Hello!* Vale, sorry, but there's not much choice, really.

▮ V: Ballard is dead [2009], so "Death Becomes

You" (... but not now, please!).

■ LL: I AM Death.

▮ V: So how about Lydia as the female Ballard?

■ LL: I'm all for it.

▮ V: People in my little cultural niche, we're all wondering, "Now that Burroughs and Ballard are dead—who can we trust?" Well?

■ LL: [smiling] I dunno...would *I* trust me? Hmmm... a gal's gotta eat! Look, we've had so many great conversations at this table that I pity you for having to transcribe—

▮ V: Yeah, and we aren't done. We used to be in the Ballardian mode and now we'll be in the Lydian mode, which is actually a musical term for a certain scale—

■ LL: I know what it is: it's the Chord of the Devil, damned by the Church... I'm not saying another word until I get a *cookie*. I wish I had a copy of my cookbook to give you, because, you know, I just did my cookbook: *The Need to Feed*—

▮ V: You did a cookbook?!

■ LL: I did everything!

▮ V: These cookies are sugar-free, which is a miracle—

■ LL: Don't ruin my fun. These are *dee-lish!* I have a very nice recipe in my cookbook for Chocolate Avocado Mousse: organic cocoa powder, avocado, vanilla, and agave; no cooking, no flour, no eggs, no sugar. Mix well, cool, eat. It's very sassy. I'll be doing a reading in New York for the book. I did a reading in Ojai—

▮ V: Ojai, California?!

■ LL: Yeah.

▮ V: That's the birthplace of all these *cults* in California—

■ LL: I'm trying to start my own. So far there's one member: you!

▮ V: Well, that's a good idea, actually: start a church.

■ LL: I have my own church. Only myself and Ian White, the drummer of Big Sexy Noise are members.

▮ V: Churches are so good because then everyone can give you tax-deductible contributions—

■ LL: Once we hire the secretary, we will have a tax return.

▮ V: And you get breaks on rent; there's a million deductions if you're a church.

■ LL: Absolutely true. And that's why I signed up at the Universal Life Church. From now on, it's the *Reverend Lydia Lunch* to you. I *am* the Universal Church.

▮ V: But you can also start your own church.

■ LL: Exactly. But first, I'd have to kill you.

▮ V: The Church of the Lydian Lunch! [laughs]

■ LL: It's the Church of the Sexually Insane—

it's been going for quite a few years.
∎ V: Oh, *there's* a concept—

∎ LL: Come on Vale, this is not new to you! You know I end my Spoken Word pieces with my big crescendo of "Welcome to MY Church—where there is only one commandment: REBELLION FROM FALSE VIRTUE. The only real rebellion is *pleasure* because it's the first thing they stole from us in the first f--king place." If you haven't heard this, you haven't heard anything. And you probably *haven't* heard it because I can't afford to do my Spoken Word shows in this country anymore [slams hand on table].

■ ■ ■

You know, in the day of high technology, technology does not *really* make our life easier: it steals our time, makes time go faster, wastes an incredible amount of time, and benefits *what?* Who? Well, certainly there *is* a benefit—but I am a Luddite!

▍V: Yeah, *who* does it benefit? That's a good question.

■ LL: It can be incredibly time-sucking *and* accelerating at the same time. Because where has time gone since technology has accelerated? Into the rabbit hole. Because so much time gets evaporated into the vacuum that is technology, where there is no real communication, where there is no real knowledge, where there is just the repetition of pointless facts, where you can find everything and learn nothing. That's the problem with youth today. That's why they should all be shot, killed, and barbecued. [Imitates a person getting shot; struggling to get words out] "Hallelujah! Hallelujah! Hallelujah!" Message to the youth: That is the Church of the Lydian Mode.

▍V: Hey, do you know Genesis P-Orridge?

■ LL: ...I have met Genesis a few times. I think he's a great writer and has some good ideas... I think he's got a brilliant mind and he should write more... In *Apocalypse Culture* [1990], there are some essays that were so good.

Let's review for a minute—in the early part of the evening out of your mouth came J.G. Ballard and at the end of the evening out of your mouth comes Genesis P-Orridge. Let's not confuse the two with anything to do with *me!*

RECENT SHOWS

■ V: That was the most intense show I've seen YOU do, Lydia. I love that long piece at the end, which is like a Voodoo trance—

■ LL: "Black Juju"? Alice Cooper did that song. We mutated it a little. I'm glad to hear it's the most intense show of my career—thanks. That was our second show. We only had *two* rehearsals because of Hurricane Sandy. The band rehearsed without me, obviously. Algis lives in Brooklyn.

■ V: Weasel Walter on guitar lived here in Oakland?

■ LL: He played drums in Burmese last time we were here as Teenage Jesus and the Jerks, at Slim's [San Francisco venue]. He's damn good, isn't he? He's good.

■ V: I like the way he "freaked out" at the end.

■ LL: He's a freaky dork.

▮ V: I noticed that you two [Lydia and Algis] had what appeared to be charts on music stands, but Weasel Walter didn't.

■ LL: Yeah, we had our charts—*I* had all my lyrics.

▮ V: Yeah, your lyrics. I figured it was like an outline/reminder.

■ LL: Of course, because we only had two rehearsals together.

▮ V: You know, it is very tricky to get your voice to always be decipherable—with *any* band. I noticed you had Eugene trying to put pressure on the sound man to enhance your vocals—

■ LL: Yeah, I had Eugene as my "sound bodyguard"—cuz if my voice is buried—

▮ V: I don't know why the human voice usually gets drowned out by the band; I don't get that.

■ LL: Have you seen the size of this guy [points to Algis] or heard the sound of his bass? Vocals and bass are on different frequencies, but I'm really in the bass frequency a lot now. I mean, my voice has dropped. Next year, only dogs will hear me.

I did a show recently in London with this group called the Tin-Tone Army. It was seven tin guitars ["sonic fascinators"]—they were like lunch boxes—the sound was incredible. Some lunch boxes could open and inside would be flowers, or, the guy that makes them [Jon Free] says he carries his underwear on tour in the lunchbox. I will be gifted one, I am very happy to say, at Christmas, when I go back to do another performance with the Tin-Tone Army. Go on their website [www.tin-tone.com]: these guitars are amazing. They play everything from Motörhead to Hank Williams. It's a lunch box with a neck, and there's seven of them and they have two female drummers—one played a trashcan lid and one like just hid behind. The lead singer is from Philly—long-haired hippie. I sang "All Tomorrow's Parties" [Velvet Underground] and "Death Valley '69" [Sonic Youth] with them.

Tin-Tone Army: these guitars are *beautiful,* so good, the sound is great live—it's hard to capture, but there are some videos. And they're all unique. He's made hundreds of these guitars out of lunch boxes. Tin-Tone Army: highly recommended! [claps hands]

I'm debuting my Cypress Grove "Desert Blues" in an old fabric/textile factory that's been converted into art spaces; it's opening at the end of September. It's really beautiful—it's "Meet My Inner Bobbie Gentry."

I'm working with this video artist and we just finished a video yesterday on the "burn zone" between Spain and France. We're doing this "Desert Blues" band and are projecting behind it videos of the ghost towns we've been going to. It's like turning a Spaghetti Western on its head—instead of blood and bullets, the *desert* is the star. Yeah, really gorgeous. I'm gonna send you a link to some of the—not really *music videos,* but *illustrated songs* that we did videos to. We went up to where there was a huge fire on the border and did a beautiful video that's going to be the backdrop to a Mark Lanegan song that we cover. So, you know, good stuff like that!

▮ V: You've adopted this huge, affordable video projection technology which is pretty recent—

■ LL: Yeah. Also, the woman I'm working with is just amazing. We got back Monday night and by Wednesday night she'd edited this three-minute video of the burn zone. She's my new collaborative partner and we've done a bunch of things in the past six months. It's funny, because she came to visit me and I said, "We better make some films, because this won't last too much longer," as I pointed to my face [laughs].

▮ V: What do you mean? You could always be like the star of *Eyes Without a Face* and wear that haunting mask!

■ LL: Anna Magnani. [editor's note: the actress was actually Edith Scob]

■ V: Oh, yeah! I just saw her in *Roma,* her last film performance. Fellini caught her entering her apartment building at night and filmed her.

■ LL: Yeah, amazing. Well, they just showed *The Fugitive Kind.* They have really great morning cable TV here. Usually at 7 a.m. (which is when I'm waking up after going to sleep at 3:30 a.m.), there's a really good classic on. And *The Fugitive Kind* with Marlon Brando and Anna Magnani was on the other day, and it was fantastic.

■ V: Wow. I gotta see that.

■ LL: *Somebody* has got to *represent,* you know—these are the *real* women! They exist in society, and I guess that still falls on my shoulders! So, there ya go; I'm not goin' away. I'm not gonna shut up.

■ V: You better not. Let the others die young! We want you to last till you're 100, like Leni Riefenstahl. You could be the Leni Riefenstahl of *our side.*

■ LL: Well, if it's tomorrow or if it's in 40 years, it doesn't matter; I've made my skidmark on the face of history, so... eat my dust!

BABIES & CHILDREN

We had a very nice experience on the plane

where I had to bounce a 14-lb sausage up and down for an hour—oh, I mean, *a young baby*. Weasel was sitting next to a mother whose baby was crying and I'm like, *"Please, let me take over,"* because I *do* have that talent of silencing babies. So I'm just doing what I naturally do to a child, which is to try to shake it to death: [demon rasp] "Agh! Agh! Agh! Agh!" banging its head up and down. The child loved me, of course, because I was just doing what *it* naturally wanted me to do. And I'm, like, *EXTREME*. It was an energy exchange.

Usually, I hypnotize them and they instantly silence—it's my *forte*. So, this little bag of meat was just going—it was bordering on autistic. I was teaching it "Red Alert" [drumming on table] *nah-nah-nah-nah...* And every time I tried to give it back to its mother, "WAH" —I had to take it back. For the benefit of the plane, really—this is what I *have* to do; it's the only thing I do for free, and I'm very good at it. The mother is like impressed... But, at the end, when the plane stopped and I gave it back, the baby cried the final "WAH!" because it was just like sad... and I left! Once I'm done with 'em, I'm done with 'em. Like, "I'm really sorry, but I'm gonna give it back to ya!"

▌ V: [laughs]

■ LL: But, you know, I was blessed with this talent in Italy. When I went to pick up Connie Burg (No Wave artist, aka China Burg; aka Lucy Hamilton) one day—she was staying in a villa for some No Wave performance… I went to pick her up and twenty children surrounded me. I had bright red hair at the time so I thought they thought I was Bozo the Clown. They surrounded me and all wanted to dance and sing with me, and they bestowed upon me, at that moment (or so I philosophize), this *gift*. And the gift was to be able to silence a child within five seconds of it screaming—and this is *extremely* handy on a plane or a train.

Now, I usually don't dedicate a f—king *hour* of my life to a little screaming tantrum-izer because you know how I feel about children: *they should be obscene and not heard.* But today, however, the sausage monster… (I did literally bang its head twice on the ceiling but it didn't even cry.)

▮ V: Maybe the ceilings are padded—

■ LL: But I'm telling you, I have this gift… it's mysterious, because I will never s—t one out. I think it's very unnatural: *childbirth!* I think there is nothing more repulsive, painful, horrible, or abusive than childbirth. I feel that if it doesn't fit in, it shouldn't come out! I don't believe in it one bit. However... I can silence the little lepers.

▮ V: But it's so much fun doing the deed that produces a child—see, there's some unfairness there.

■ LL: Well, some of you breeders have done a good job; others should *know better.* Because *mine* would just be all [demon rasp] "AGGHHH!"— The Exorcist! [Devil's child] I don't think it would be fair to carry on the line after I'm gone.

But it's a beautiful thing, to have this hypnosis toward children. And usually it's the *fathers* that get scared—they're like, "What the f—k is going on here?!" And I'm like, "I'm talking— *please."* This was one baby on a plane that could have been *sacrificed.*

DEATH & HEALING

▮ V: [laughs] "Oh, it's dead. *Sorry!"* You know, I hate to say this but I saw the murder of a dog in Washington Square Park.

■ LL: Oh! [saddened]

▮ V: There was one of those tiny, little, trendy, yappy dogs in the park.

■ LL: Yep, that everyone has—

▮ V: —that a lot of yuppie-types have—

■ LL: A yuppie-yapper—I hate it! A yuppie-yapper, it's horrible.

▌V: But this other more serious, more *gravitas* dog came up and—

■ LL: Tore it to pieces?

▌V: No—in one fell swoop it snapped its neck.

■ LL: And it was dead?!

▌V: Well, it wasn't *quite* dead—

■ LL: Even worse!

▌V: The naïve couple said—and I wanted to tell them, *"You fools! This dog just killed your dog!"* But I didn't say that—

■ LL: Oh my god, they didn't know? They didn't even know!

▌V: No—they were so clueless. They just said,

"Sunset over Belchite" by Lydia Lunch

111

"Oh, he's sick!"

■ LL: He's "sick"?!

▮ V: Well, Marian heard them say, "Well, he isn't bleeding," but I didn't hear that line. I just told them where the nearest vet was and I saw them hailing a cab, but I knew that it was dead already.

■ LL: Oh well, you see—that's terrible! I would *never* hurt an animal.

▮ V: Only a human animal! But there are too many of those!

■ LL: Don't put words in my mouth.

▮ V: [laughs]

■ LL: You have to know how to speak the language of the killer you are against. In my opinion, small dogs are cute—it's what you should have in the city: to be kind to your neighbors. You have small apartments, small dogs are good. But dogs, in general, are killers. [mock contemplative tone:] What is death? What is death, but a transitory state of being. "Death"—does it really exist? This is what I fear: I do not fear death, I fear that there *is no death.* This is the trauma.

You see, most people are frightened to die; I am frightened to live beyond death. I'm not frightened [of death] because I've come to terms with it—recycling and all that s—t. But beyond death: What if there is no death?! I mean: remaining mentally conscious beyond death. Energy cannot be disintegrated, however, it does transform, so: what happens to the consciousness?! The worst, I think, would be just: *the floating mind.* [laughs] Because I've *been* in that state before and it was horrible.

■ V: Okay, I'll give you my thought.

■ LL: Please.

■ V: Which is that word *"liminal."* I looked it up last night—because that's a word that has no hold on my mind—and the example given is: a state of transitoriness or transition. They gave an example "as between life and death." And I thought, *What the f—k?! A transition state that's between life and death?* Liminal—not *sub*-liminal. Liminal refers to any transition state between "a" and "b."

■ LL: Well, my nearest experience with that state was to wake up during surgery, and be floating above my body, in a state of—well, a comatose state, but where I was conscious and couldn't physically move or talk. There has been a TV series on this actually, recently. When this happened to *me,* which was twenty years ago, nobody was talking about it. I woke up during surgery, floating above my body in such agony that I could not express, because the anesthesia had worn off. So I could *hear* the doctors talking, and I could *see* the operation, and I could

113

feel intense f--king agony for which I could not voice—*this* was f--king hell.

▮ V: You're not the only person who has—

■ LL: I know that! This is because anesthesia is not a precise, exact science. It can cause a great amount of trauma—

▮ V: —and even brain damage. They make big bucks, these anesthesiologists. It's such a delicate practice—between an art and a science.

■ LL: It was sheer, incredible, physical agony with no voice—I think, with the shock of pain, which becomes so immense that you just have to come back down to your body—you cast yourself out. But, I've seen specials on this and people say that it has just traumatized them for their entire life. Because, of course surgery is never safe, but you go in with unlimited trust and some people come out and they just can't *deal.* They're no longer in pain, but they're in this... not liminal and not limbo—

▮ V: —a "liminal limbo"!

■ LL: I was having, like, serious surgery, and I'm looking down at it, and I'm just beseeching every god, goddess, demon, to just... I don't know how long I was floating above, but the pain—just to be in it temporarily was intense. But I came back. So "All right, I'm back—now give me the f--king morphine!" It's just another one of those *landmarks* that differentiates me from most of the rest of the human race.

▮ V: Did you ever read a book titled *Blindness?*

■ LL: I loved it! José Saramago. That was a *really* good book. Yeah, he just died [June 18, 2010].

▮ V: He got a Nobel Prize in Literature, 1998.

■ LL: A whole town goes blind, I don't know why! [laughs] But it's a really great book.

▮ V: Right! And there's another book—I can't think of the title now—written by a guy who wrote his book by blinking.

■ LL: Blinking?!

▮ V: He was totally paralyzed, but somehow, by blinking, he managed to—

■ LL: —write a book?! Oh, Jesus. Unbelievable.

▮ V: It's suffocating and it's short; it's not really long. [*The Diving Bell and the Butterfly* by Jean-Dominique Bauby.]

■ LL: So, the book *itself* is a suffocation? [laughs] A suffocating experience of endurance.

▮ V: Yeah. I got it from the library; I don't own it.

■ LL: Sideways to this story: in France, if you have burns and you go to the hospital burn ward, they ask you immediately, "Do you want us to call the 'fire man'?" [a French term for psychic healer]. In France, they do psychic healings for burns and people really believe that it works—if people say "Yes," it turns out they have a much better rate of reparation. Only in France have I heard that for the burn unit, they call in "healers."

THE FIELD

By the way, I want to recommend the *best* book I've read in years. It's called *The Field* by Lynne McTaggart. It's about "Zero Point Field" [*The Field* pp.19-24] which—Einstein said—is that spooky stuff between distances. It's not about the black void, it's not about vacuum, it's not about gravity, it's about the connective tissue of electromagnetic information that connects everything.

Her previous book was called *What Doctors Won't Tell You.* This is one of the best books I've read in years: *The Field*. She interviewed a hundred scientists—astronauts… The first 30 pages took me about four months, then it got faster. It's a lot about quantum physics. It's not that it's *technical*, it's that you first have to wrap your mind around the concepts. But then they go into, for example, in one experiment they asked, "Where does memory live? The brain? The mind? Outside the mind? Outside the body? The collective, universal hard drive that is the

Universe?" Zero Point Field...

They took salamanders—and salamanders can, you know, grow back their arms and we can't. They cut a salamander's brain in half because they were trying to find where memory lives. So, they cut the brain in half: salamander still had memory. They cut the brain in 3/4: salamander still had memory. They scrambled—*literally* [imitates blender sound]—the salamander's brains and put them back in scrambled. The salamanders still had memory. They could also *still* grow back their arms—which the scientists can't figure out; science has *not* figured out how.

■ V: If they could transpose those genes to humans—

■ LL: We know DNA—but we don't know how the cells tell each other. And this is it: *the secret language of the cells is a fetish of mine.* So with salamander experimentation, they're trying to figure out why a salamander can grow back an arm and we can't; why a cell knows to make an arm and a hand—we can't decode that.

So two scientists decide Zero Point Field is the thing they're investigating. Because if we can hook into that field, it can power space travel which is now powered by nuclear power. Again, Zero Point Field is that spooky stuff between distances, which suggests everything is connected,

100%. Memory living outside the brain—because it's a collective, universal, connective tissue of magnetism. Zero Point Field: that's where the hard drive is [*The Field* p.90]. So, at first no one was interested. But Zero Point Field is now, like, Number 2 on the Pentagon's list of research. Because if we can tap into *that,* then we can have powered space travel and everything else [*The Field* p.30].

Every chapter is quite different—like, there was one chapter, for instance, about light in the body [*The Field* p.40 +]. One doctor said there is light in the body and he was just laughed at: "What do you mean, there is light in the body?!"

▮ V: Bioluminescence.

■ LL: Exactly. So a student comes to him and says, "Help me get my Ph.D." The doctor says, "Help me prove there is light in the body." Student goes, "I will prove there *isn't* light in the body." Doctor says, "Fine, I'll help you get your Ph.D." So, they start with a cucumber seed and they conclude, "Well, *of course* it has power from the sun, so there is gonna be light in a cucumber seed. Okay, we'll go to a potato." [*The Field* p.42]

Of course, a potato is also organic. So they devise a copper-lined room—completely copper, the darkest room you've ever invented—and keep going up the food chain: cucumber seed, potato… Well, of course it's plant life. So now, let's bring the *bodies* inside, and of course there's light coming out of the f--king body, because that's what we all are—energy, light, matter: it's all connected [*The Field* p.44]. So, we're losing a lot of light out into the universe. And with light coming out of the body, where is it going and what is it doing? And what exactly does it mean?

Let's go now to homeopathy and whether it works or not (these are just chapter after chapter). The miniscule molecular structure of any *essence* makes up homeopathy when diluted into water to the nth degree… so it's evaporated now and the molecule no longer exists, but it exists

"The Body as Battlefield" by Lydia Lunch

in water because *water has memory*. No one believed in homeopathy at first; they said, "Okay, let's do 105 trials" and three of four labs [or 81 trials] got positive results with the homeopathy [*The Field* p.71]. One doctor said that homeopathy is bullsh-t, so they studied the doctor, and it turned out that the doctor's *magnetism* was f--king with the studies—the doctor's magnetism, or light, or energy—whatever you wanna f--king call it—was *altering* the studies!

▮ V: The Heisenberg Uncertainty Principle: the act of observing alters that which is being observed—

■ LL: —which is quantum physics... so, *the observer alters.* And this is what they've done with particle studies.

▮ V: Believe Nothing. Doubt Everything.

■ LL: You can study the language of a cell—and this is why I say *the only democracy left is bacteria:* because bacteria starts as a single cell, and when it multiplies to a certain community it takes a vote on whether it's going to become benign or malignant. This is not *my* theory, this has been proven: it's the secret language of the cells. And if you wanna get down to minutiae, let's go even beyond minutiae—let's go to the *minute* minutiae of the invisibility of cells and their secret language which drives everything...

Bacteria responds to psychic energy.

■ V: Probably *everything* does.

■ LL: There's been over 100 studies of people doing *remote curing* for cancer: when people who had cancer didn't know they were being cured. The studies covered different people with different kinds of whatever-you-want-to-call-it. This is not in the book *The Field,* this is from my friend who lives in France and tells me that if anyone wants to call in the healers, they don't even have to come there—they can heal *remotely.*

France also has very good hospice care for AIDS patients: a very gentle way of treating people that have all kinds of afflictions. There's a great book written about the way the French treat dying people: *Intimate Death* [by Marie de Hennezel]. And it's written by a crew of doctors who decided to make an AIDS hospice for people to die a good death even though they have a horrible disease. To die a good death: a knowledgeable, a conscious, a comfortable death. Because the worst thing about death is *fear*—especially the family's fear—and greed for life. It's called *Intimate Death.* Anyway, just some thoughts.

■■■

A RE/Search Pocketbook

Reading at Moe's, Berkeley

PHILOSOPHY & DNA

Write this down, please: Picosecond Program-
mable Laser scanner: you will s—t yourself. It's
a device they're gonna have at the airports to
read your *molecules* to tell what's IN them, instead of the body scanners. *We are doomed. This
country is condemned.* Welcome to America, A--
hole! (I was smart enough to move out.) Two
years' time, it'll be here: "Okay, we no longer
have to scan you at the airport." "Oh, isn't it
going to be a lot faster?! (blurrrrp) Oh, okay."
So, it can *read your molecules:* the last time you
did drugs, what you ate for breakfast: "Bacon!"

[chants/hits table rhythmically] *"We Are Doomed. We Are Doomed."*

If you want to know more of my philosophy, it's within this book [*Will Work for Drugs*]. It's essays. There are interviews with four of my favorite writers: Hubert Selby, Jerry Stahl, an article on Ron Athey, and Nick Tosches. Intro is by Karen Finley—she's great. The cover photo was taken in an alley in Barcelona. You want some of my montages—especially my self-portrait: the soldier with the machine gun over my face—that's what you need.

TECH & POLITICS

■ V: You're full of these amazing lines, like: "I've made my skidmark on the dust of history."

■ LL: I have a few of *your* books scattered around my living room. People are always manhandling them... I have to wipe them off every time someone leaves!

■ V: Everyone has gotten so much more "visual culture"-oriented—i.e., they don't have the rigor to read anything longer than 2 pages anymore.

■ LL: Well, hasn't it been a successful experiment in reducing people's vision and scope down to a 2-inch by 2-inch screen that they hold in their hand? I mean, hasn't that been a success-ful experiment in *technological slavery?*

▮ V: Amen! That's beautiful, Lydia.

■ LL: I pat myself on my own back—I know what rolls off my tongue, honey! So move over, 'cuz here comes Big Sister!

L to R: Jello Biafra, Lydia Lunch, V. Vale

▮ V: Yes! Molten gold and singing silver rolls off your tongue—

■ LL: We need to be propping each other up in this period—it's such a brutal and heinous time in history. It's that all of these motherf--kers have gotten so much more *arrogant.* I mean, not that I cornered the market on arrogance, but holy s—t! The arrogance of the duplicitous nature of the homicidal machine that is America is just awe-inspiring.

■ V: Yeah! And "awe" is not a complimentary word these days.

■ LL: No, it isn't. Absolutely not. I say that with no sense of glory. And the "beige puppet" isn't making matters any better—as I call yo' President. Hallelujah! Louis Farrakhan, I'm talkin'! Farrakhan had some good speeches about our brotha' Barack Obama: "There is a murderer in the White House! An assassin!" Yeah, you should look up the Farrakhan speeches; just Google, "Farrakhan + Murderer in the White House"— inspirational.

■ V: Wow. Great.

■ LL: How long have I been saying: it should be the end of the "White Man's Revolution"?! Twenty years out of my mouth. Now, if the "beige puppet" would only grow some f--king balls—and those balls are black—I was saying this last night: *Grow some motherf--king balls, bitch!* This has just been a helluva four years.

■ V: *Message to Obama:* Lean on those Wall Street criminals and Too-Big-To-Fail Banks—

■ LL: You know, I pity you people here! I pity you U.S. citizens. I pity you fools that didn't do as I did, which was to leave under the *second thievery* of the Bush Administration. But, always being one step ahead of the fray and—obviously, I don't have much to move because I sell everything...

SEASONAL INSANITY

■ LL: I'm gonna close this up with a little detail that I've just learned in these times of death and dying which surround us all; so many people are dying. I was starting to wonder why I'm always more insane in the summer than I am at any other time of the year. So I started a Google self-analysis search, 'cuz I was born in the summer.

Now, my house was kind of the center point of the riots of 1967 in Rochester, New York. On July 23, 1967, I know that at the age of eight I was standing, in the summer, on the second floor of our house in the ghetto, when sudden light, and the dust motes contained within it, hit what can only be described as my "third eye," illustrating that my life was not only *not normal,* but that I was living with a maniac (also known as my father).

Okay, *there's always a third thing,* of course. So, I'm revisiting my own history, trying to figure out this *summer* situation, and I go back a little further. I'm eight years old: riots of '67. Six years old: consciousness hits me. Five years old:

the riots of 1964—which are historical in American history, because they were some of the worst: a thousand people were arrested, a helicopter crashed a few blocks from my house, twenty people were killed in the three-day conflagration that also began July 23rd or 24th; once more my house was like the *epicenter* of the rioting. *And I just figured this out.*

I mean, I knew about these riots; it was right up to the Civil Rights Act, the passing of anti-Segregation into law—but, because I concentrated on the riots of '67 when I was eight years old and thought it gave me my *spirit of rebellion and protest* that I always had—hitting upon the riots of 1964, I thought, "Well, was I just in a *war zone* for three years of my life?!" I just thought it was *one* thing but it was really *two:* I had the war inside my own home and I had the war outside my front door. And after realizing this, and going on Google Street View and looking in my own backyard (a *good* use of technology, right?), I thought, "Well maybe *now* I have the handle on my insanity that always seems to come in the summer." Yeah!

▪ V: It's very rare that we think about how we might be "controlled" by time or by seasons—

■ LL: Well, I'm very aware of all that. Anniversaries—*invisible anniversaries:* the cells remember, the body remembers; the body bears the burden of trauma. I mean, to a five-year old, you know: my father screaming, "Where's my shotgun?!" like he's going to *take on* the situation, as one of the only white families in a black ghetto, that had no choice but to *rebel,* you know, considering the circumstances... Um, yeah, I'm much better, as you can tell. Sanity has returned! HA! HA! HA! "She laughs like a madwoman."

■ ■ ■

Lydia Lunch partial cv

EXHIBITIONS

2006

Ecstasy at the Mouth of the Abyss. Galerie Kennory Kim, Paris, France. Solo exhibition.

2004

YOU ARE NOT SAFE IN YOUR OWN HOME. With Marc Viaplana. FIERCE Festival, Birmingham, England. Installation.

THE SCENE OF THE CRIME COULD BE ANYWHERE AT ANYTIME. With Marc Viaplana. FIERCE Festival, Birmingham, England. Installation.

1998

Gallery Luscombe, San Francisco, CA. Mixed media.

La Luz De Jesus, Los Angeles, CA. Mixed media.

Zenith Gallery, Pittsburgh, PA. Mixed media.

La Musardine, Paris, France. Photography.

Gandy Gallery, Prague, Czech Republic. Photography.

1997

Tribal Act, Paris, France. Photography.

Pez-Ner, Lyon, France. Photography.

Effenar, Eindhoven, Holland. Photography.

New Image Art Gallery, Los Angeles, CA. Photography.

Harold & Maude's, Orlando, FL. Photography.

2-South Gallery, Detroit, MI. Photography.

1995

Rita Dean Gallery, San Diego, CA. Photography.

SPOKEN WORD

2004

"Time of Dying." United States and European Tour.

FILM WORK

2009

Blank City, dir. Celine Danheir. Interviewed.

No Wave - Underground '80 Berlin-New York, dir. Christoph Dreher.

For The End of Time, dir. Ema Kugler. Narrator.

Post Apocalyptic Cowgirls, dir. Maria Beatty. Composer.

2008

Death of the Reel, dir. Benjamin Meade. Narrator.

2007

Real Pornography, dir. Ludovic Cantais. La Luna Films. Documentary on the artist.

Llik Your Idols, dir. Angélique
  Bosio. Interviewed.
Santa Cruz County Anti-Meth
  Campaign PSA, dir. Cam
  Archer. Narrator.

2006

Kill Your Idols, dir. Scott A.
  Crary. Interviewed.

2005

*American Fame Pt. 2: Forgetting
  Jonathan Brandis,* dir. Cam
  Archer. Narrator.

2004

*American Fame Pt. 1: Drowning
  River Phoenix,* dir. Cam
  Archer. Narrator.
*The Heart Is Deceitful Above All
  Things,* dir. Asia Argento.
  Cameo appearance,
  photography.

2002

D.I.Y. OR DIE, dir. Michael W.
  Dean. Interviewed.

2000

Shadow Hours, dir. Isaac H.
  Eaton. Scene writer,
  consultant.

1997

Girls Girls Girls, dir. Ellen Maki.
  Performance.

1996

Visiting Desire, dir. Beth B.
  Acted.

1995

Power of the Word, dir. Jeanne
  Harco. Appearance.

1992

Malicious Intent, dir. Richard
  Kern & Chris Lovenko.
  Spoken word
  performance.
The Thunder, The Perfect Mind,
  dir. Tom Richards Murphy
  and Marta Ze. Acted,
  narrated.

1990

BBQ Death Squad from Hell, dir.
  Penn & Teller. Acted.
Kiss Napoleon Goodbye, dir.
  Babeth Mondini & Lydia
  Lunch. Acted, wrote, co-
  directed.
Thanatopsis, dir. Beth B. Acted,
  wrote.
The Road To God Knows Where,
  dir. Uli M. Schüppel.
  Cameo appearance.

1983

The Cutting Edge, MTV.
  Appeared in 6 episodes.

1988

The Gun Is Loaded, dir. Merrill
  Aldighieri & Joe Tripician.
  Acted, wrote.

1987

Submit To Me Now, dir by
  Richard Kern. Acted
Put More Blood Into The Music,
  dir. George Atlas.
  Interviewed.
Mondo New York, dir. Harvey
  Keith. Appearance.

1986

Fingered, dir. Richard Kern.

Acted, wrote.

The Invisible Thread, dir. Penn & Teller. Acted.

Gang of Souls, dir. Maria Beatty. Interviewed.

1985

Submit To Me, dir. Richard Kern. Acted.

The Right Side of My Brain, dir. Richard Kern. Acted, wrote.

1983

Vortex, dir. Beth B & Scott B. Acted.

The Wild World of Lydia Lunch, dir. Nick Zedd. Acted.

Like Dawn To Dust, dir. Vivenne Dick. Acted, wrote.

1980

Liberty's Booty, dir. Vivienne Dick. Acted.

The Offenders, dir. Beth B & Scott B. Acted.

1979

Beauty Becomes The Beast, dir. Vivienne Dick. Acted.

Alien Portrait, dir. Michael McClard. Performance.

1978

Guerillere Talks, dir. Vivienne Dick. Acted.

Black Box, dir. Beth B & Scott B. Acted.

She Had Her Gun All Ready, dir. Vivienne Dick. Acted.

Rome '78. dir. James Nares. Acted.

PLAYS

1990

The Smell of Guilt, with Emilio Cubeiro. Dance Theatre Workshop 10th Anniversary, New York. Co-wrote, acted, directed, produced.

1988

South of Your Border, with Emilio Cubeiro. New Theatre, New York. Co-wrote, acted, directed, produced.

BIBLIOGRAPHY

2012

The Need to Feed. Cookbook. Universe.

2009

Will Work For Drugs. Introduction by Karen Finley. Akashic Books.

Amnesia. Poetry, photography and music. Bilingual, Contemporanea.

2008

The Gun is Loaded. Photography art book. Black Dog Publishing, UK.

Paradoxia: A Predator's Diary. Introduction by Virginie Despentes and Thurston Moore. Spanish translation. Melusina Books.

2007

Paradoxia: A Predator's Diary.
Introduction by Jerry Stahl
and Thurston Moore.
Akashic Books.

2003

Sex and Guts. Written and
edited with Gene
Gregorits. Phony Lid
Books.

1998

Toxic Gumbo. Art by Ted
McKeever. Vertigo/DC
Comics.

1997

Paradoxia: A Predator's Diary.
Introduction by Hubert
Selby, Jr. Creation Press.
French edition by La
Musardine, 1998; Czech
edition by Mata, 1999;
German edition by
Miranda Verlag, 2000;
Spanish edition, 2000;
Russian edition by
Adaptec/Tough Press,
2003; Italian edition by
Storie Press, 2005.

1993

AS-FIX-E-8, with Nick Cave, ill.
by Mike Matthews. Last
Gasp.

1992

Incriminating Evidence, ill. by
Kristian Hoffman. Last
Gasp.
Blood Sucker, ill. by Bob
Fingerman. Eros

Comix/Fantagraphics
Books.

1987

The Right Side of My Brain.
Limited Edition printing
with erotic drawings by
Knut Odde. Niels Borch
Jensen, Denmark.

1982

Adulterers Anonymous, with
Exene Cervenka. Poetry.
Grove Press, reissued in
1996 by Last Gasp.

SELECTED ARTICLES AND WRITINGS

2008

Introduction for *NO WAVE :
Post Punk. Underground.
New York. 1976–1980* by
Thurston Moore and
Byron Coley. Abrams
Image.
"The Spirit of Philosophical
Vitriol" in *Istanbul Noir*, ed.
by Mustafa Ziyalan and
Amy Spangler. Akashic
Books.

2007

"Illusive Bitch" in *Awake!: A
Reader for the Sleepless*, ed.
by Steven Lee Beeber. Soft
Skull Press.
"Johnny Behind the Deuce"
and "Real Pornography" in
*One On One: The Best
Women's Monologues for
the 21st Century*, ed. by
Joyce Henry, Rebecca

Dunn Jaroff, and Bob
Shuman. Applause Books.

2004

*Sin-A-Rama: Sleaze Sex
Paperbacks of the Sixties.*
Edited. Feral House.
"Women and Children First"
in *50 Reason NOT to Vote
for Bush.* Feral House.

2002

"Motherhood is Not
Compulsory" in
Inappropriate Behaviour.
Serpent's Tail.

1999

"Tough Love" in *Getting It* web
magazine. Weekly column.
"Original Beat/Herbert
Huncke" in *The Rolling
Stone Book of the Beats* by
Holly George-Warren.
Rolling Stone Press.
Excerpt from novel *Paradoxia.*
P.U.R.E., Vol. 1 [magazine].

1998

Excerpt from novel *Paradoxia.*
Hustler [magazine].

1997

Introduction to *Erotica Visions
Sublime,* October issue of
Juxtapoz Erotica
[magazine].
Introduction to *New York Girls*
by Richard Kern.
TASCHEN Books.
Essay on multimedia artist
Jane Handel. *Juxtapoz,* May
issue.

"Petty Intrusion" in *Noirotica II:
Pulp Friction.* Masquerade
Books.

1996–98

Ongoing contributor, *World
Arts Magazine.*

1996

Introduction to *Neurotica,* by
J.K. Potter. Overlook TP.

1995

Introduction to Ted
McKeever's graphic novel,
Metropol. Blue Eyed Dog.

1993

"Cruel Story of Youth" in *The
Girl Wants To* by Lynn
Crosbie. Coach House
Press.

1989

Introduction to *Visual
Addiction,* by Robert
Williams. Last Gasp.

1986

"Vampire's Kiss" in *Penthouse
Forum.*

1985

Text from film "Right Side of
My Brain" in *Penthouse
Forum.*

1984

Interview with Pat Benetar.
Spin Magazine.

DISCOGRAPHY

Includes solo work, group-
work, re-issues [RI], compila-

tions [C] and greatest hits
compilations [GHC].

1978

No New York [C]
Orphans / Less of Me

1979

Beirut Slump
Off White
Baby Doll/Freud in Flop/Race
    Mixing
Pink 12"EP
Pre-Teenage Jesus & The Jerks

1980

8-Eyed Spy
Queen Of Siam

1981

8-Eyed Spy
8-Eyed Spy Live
Diddy Wah Diddy
113.13

1982

Some Velvet Morning / I Fell In
    Love With A Ghost
The Agony Is The Ecstacy
Thirsty Animal
Vortex - Original Soundtrack
Der Karibische Western
Kino Aus Der Kassette
13.13

1983

Dagger & Guitar
The Last Testament

1984

Better A New Demon Than
    An Old God [C]
Plow! [C]
In Limbo

Speed Trials [C]
Death Valley '69
Hard Rock

1985

The Uncensored Lydia Lunch
Heart Of Darkness
The Drowning Of Lucy
    Hamilton
Death Valley 69 EP
Bad Moon Rising
A Dozen of Dead Roses
Tellus The Audio Cassette
    Magazine: #10 All Guitars!

1986

Hysterie [C]
Boy-Girl
Peyrere

1987

Tellus, The Audio Cassette
    Magazine #18:
    Experimental Theater

1988

Honeymoon In Red
Oral Fixation
Stinkfist
The Crumb

1989

Hysterie [GHC]
Fear, Power, God [C]
Oral Fixation Excerpts
New York Rockers
    (Manhattan's Original
    Rock Underground)
Zetrospective, Vol. I: Dancing
    in the Face of Adversity

1990

Conspiracy Of Women
    (COW)

Our Fathers Who Aren't In
  Heaven
Naked In Garden Hills
Stinkfist & The Crumb [RI]
Girl Doesn't Get Killed By A
  Make-Believe Lover...'Cuz
  It's Hot

1991

Trying To Make It To The End
  Of The Century
Don't Fear The Reaper
POW
Shotgun Wedding
Queen of Siam [RI]
Spooky
King of the Jews

1992

Head On
Downtown Does The Beatles
Twisted

1993

Sweat
Shotgun Wedding Live
Unearthly Delights
Queen of Siam [RI]
Welcome to My Nightmare
  (Tribute to Alice Cooper)
Fear Engine II: Almost As If IT
  Never Happened
13 Above the Night
Workdogs In Hell [C]

1994

Unhealthy
Crimes Against Nature
Transmutation & Shotgun
  Wedding Live

1995

Teenage Jesus & The Jerks -
  EVERYTHING

1995 The Drowning Of Lucy
  Hamilton / In Limbo
1995 Rude Hieroglyphics
1995 Arkkon

1996

Uncensored / Oral Fixation
  [RI]
Universal Infiltrators
Home Alive [C]
Flesh, Fangs & Filigree [C]:
  "Stinkfist"
Flesheaters [C]: "In My Time
  of Dying"
Undead [C]: "Twisted" &
  "Some Velvet Morning"
Stinkfist /Meltdown
  Oratorio/Son of Stink/ The
  Crumb
No Excuse
Out of Their Mouths, MK. 2 -
  An Atavistic Compilation
Mind the Gap Vol. 9

1997

Kiss of the Vampire [C]
Necromantic [C]: "In My Time
  of Dying"
Tribute To Jack Kerouac [C]
8-Eyed Spy "Luncheone"
The Desperate Ones
York
Grrrl Power: A History of
  Women in Popular Music
Stiletto Vamp [C]: "Burning
  Skulls"
Kerouac: Kicks Joy Darkness
Vital Juices
Dead & Gone #2: Totenlieder

1998

Here: Brooklyn Bank
Gothic Erotica [C]: "Stinkfist",

"Burning Skulls"
Before the Balloon Went Up
    [C]: "In My Time of Dying"
U Turn
Matrikamantra
Queen of Siam [IR]
Songs of the Witchblade [C]
Widowspeak [GHC]
Crippled Champions [C],
    "Escape"
Honeymoon In Red
Il Juke-Box Del Diavolo
Crippled Champions: The
    Soundtrack Generation

1999

Radio History of KBUR FM
    [C], reading from
    "Paradoxia"
Crimes Against Nature [IR]
Original Soundtrack: The Blair
    Witch Project
Shotgun Wedding / Shotgun
    Wedding Live
Yesterday's Zeitgeist
Shotgun Wedding
Dirty Little Secrets - Music to
    Strip By...
Re-Up
Drinking from Puddles
Education In Infestation
Kaleidoscope 6

2000

New Coat of Paint
Rotunda
Ontogeny - No Fish Is Too
    Weird for Her Aquarium
    (vol. II)
The Devil's Racetrack
Beauty and Terror

2001

Hangover Hotel
Downtown '81 (original
    soundtrack)

2002

Champagne, Cocaine &
    Nicotine Stains
Blue Light Fever
"&"
Wake The Dead: Words &
    Music from Sex and Guts
The Sound of Il Giaguaro Vol 2
Electric Jazz Vol. I
Nu Jazz Vol. 3

2003

In Our Time of Dying
Memory and Madness
Exploding Plastic Pleasure
Queer Street (No Fish Is Too
    Weird for Her Aquarium
    Vol. III)

2004

Smoke In The Shadows
Live in London

2005

Operett Amorale
Sartorial Sampler
Willing Victim - The Audience
    as Whipping Boy
No New York [C]

2006

Smoke in the Shadows / Lost
    World / Blame / Pass Like
    Night
Teenage Jesus and the Jerks
    Live at Max's Kansas City
    1977
Touch My Evil
Protocol
CBGB's ("Orphans")